TO PREACH THE TRUTH

To Preach the Truth

SELECTED SERMONS AND HOMILIES

Schubert M. Ogden

 CASCADE *Books* · Eugene, Oregon

TO PREACH THE TRUTH
Selected Sermons and Homilies

Cascade Books
An Imprint of Wipf and Stock Publishers
199 W. 8th Ave., Suite 3
Eugene, OR 97401

www.wipfandstock.com

ISBN: 978-1-62564-943-0

Cataloging-in-Publication data:

Ogden, Schubert M.

    To preach the truth : selected sermons and homilies / Schubert M. Ogden.

    x + 156 p. ; 23 cm.

    ISBN: 978-1-62564-943-0

    1. Sermons. 2. Sermons, American. 3. Methodist Church—Sermons. I. Title.

BX5937 O35 2015

Manufactured in the USA

The author thanks those who have generously granted permission to make use of
previously published material: "'Every One Who Is of the Truth . . . '" (26 Janu-
ary 1955), "Prudence and Grace" (6 October 1971), and "Raised with Christ: The
Meaning of the Resurrection" (16 April 1989) are all used by permission of the
Office of Communications of The Divinity School of The University of Chicago;
Dean William B. Lawrence of Perkins School of Theology, Southern Methodist
University has given permission to use "'You Also Should Do as I Have Done to
You'" (6 April 1960); "'Ask and It Will Be Given You'" (17 May 1964) first appeared
in *Rockefeller Chapel Sermons*, ed. Donovan E. Smucker (University of Chicago
Press, 1967) and is used by permission of the publisher; "'This Generation Will
Not Pass Away. . .'" (6 December 1959) was originally published in *Sermons to
Intellectuals from Three Continents*, ed. Franklin H. Littell (Macmillan 1963) and is
republished by permission of Mrs. Marcia Sachs Littell.

To all who have borne witness to me
when I have tried to bear witness to them

For this I was born, and for this I came into the world,
to bear witness to the truth.

—THE GOSPEL ACCORDING TO JOHN 18:37

Contents

CONTENTS

Preface

To be a Christian is to be called to bear witness to the truth and, in order to bear it validly, also to do theology. This is because doing theology is the form of critical reflection that asks whether bearing witness has been as valid as it claims to be and what it now has to be or become if it is to keep on being so. But this means that doing theology, as much as any other form of critical reflection, exists entirely for the sake of an activity beyond itself—in its case, the activity of bearing witness to the truth. As a Christian who has pursued the calling to do theology professionally, I have sought to bear such witness not only implicitly by all of my work as an academic theologian, but also explicitly by doing my best whenever I had "time and opportunity" both to preach the truth and to teach it as a representative minister of the church. This book and a companion volume entitled *To Teach the Truth* are offered as what I hope are fair samples of this other side of my work that the theology I've mainly done has all been intended to serve.

As for my distinction between preaching and teaching, it rests on a significant difference between two modes of bearing witness, which I distinguish as "direct" and "indirect" respectively. It is likely that something of both modes is present in most attempts to bear witness. But in any particular instance, one or the other mode may be sufficiently dominant to warrant classifying the whole accordingly. Any instance may be classified as preaching whose controlling purpose is so to proclaim the truth that God is sheer love as to call the hearer or reader directly for a personal decision: to trust in God's love and to be faithful to its cause. By contrast, any instance of bearing witness may be classified as teaching that calls for that personal decision only indirectly, in that it seeks to clarify as adequately as possible just what it means, intellectually and existentially, to make the decision in a responsible way.

What Christian preaching and teaching, so understood, have in common is that both, by their very nature, presuppose a Christian commitment. They presuppose that the preacher and the teacher alike are themselves personally committed to the truth to which they, in their different ways, are bearing witness. In this, teaching as well as preaching is to be distinguished from doing theology. For, as sure as it is that most persons who do Christian theology are like myself in doing it as a Christian calling, there's nothing logically that requires them to do so—any more than any other form of critical reflection logically requires a prior commitment to the validity of the claims on which it reflects. So it was with reason that I distinguished what is offered in this book and its companion as the "other side" of my work as one who has mainly done theology as his Christian vocation.

As it happens, the original setting in life for most, though not all, of my sermons was not local congregations, but academic communities: either those of which I was a member or others in whose chapels I was invited to preach. Since I have only rarely given titles to my sermons and homilies—other than simply to quote part or all of the texts—they are distinguished here solely by the scripture lessons containing their texts and are ordered chronologically according to the dates on which they were first preached.

In my citations from scripture, I have in almost all cases depended upon the New Revised Standard Version.

It is a joy once again to express my thanks to three friends who have been particularly helpful in completing a project: Philip E. Devenish, Franklin I. Gamwell, and Andrew D. Scrimgeour. I, of course, remain responsible for the final outcome. But I know, and my readers should know, that this is a better book because of their feedback.

Rollinsville, Colorado
October 2013

26 JANUARY 1955

John 18:33–38

Then Pilate entered the headquarters again, summoned Jesus, and asked him, "Are you the King of the Jews?" Jesus answered, "Do you ask this on your own, or did others tell you about me?" Pilate replied, "I am not a Jew, am I? Your own nation and the chief priests have handed you over to me. What have you done?" Jesus answered, "My kingdom is not from this world. If my kingdom were from this world, my followers would be fighting to keep me from being handed over to the Jews. But as it is, my kingdom is not from here." Pilate asked him, "So you are a king?" Jesus answered, "You say that I am a king. For this I was born, and for this I came into the world, to bear witness to the truth. Everyone who is of the truth hears my voice." Pilate asked him, "What is truth?"

We've heard as our New Testament lesson this morning the passage in which the author of the Fourth Gospel moves considerably beyond the account of the meeting of Jesus and Pilate that is preserved in the synoptic tradition and, in the power of the Spirit of truth, attempts to set forth the deeper significance of the encounter between Jesus and Rome. I invite you, in these moments, to consider with me the final word that the Evangelist places in Jesus' mouth: "Everyone who is of the truth hears my voice." So that we may prepare ourselves to receive whatever of God's word this text is able to mediate to us here and now, in our situation today, let us seek, first of all, to understand the meaning it has in its original context.

1

I

By far the most striking, as well as the most significant, thing about Jesus' statement is its order. He affirms, not that everyone who hears his voice is of the truth, but rather that everyone who is of the truth hears his voice. In other words, the real meaning of "hearing his voice" is "being of the truth"—or, as it's interestingly put elsewhere in the Gospel, "doing what is true" (3:21). Insofar as one is of the truth, or does what is true, there can be no question of one's hearing Jesus' voice. But—so at least the order of the statement suggests—the converse statement may not hold. There can be no guarantee that those who have heard his voice are really of the truth. To be sure, really hearing his voice is insofar being of the truth. And in this sense, his statement is indeed convertible, and one must grant that its actual order as we have it in the text would be entirely accidental were nothing but such a real hearing possible. But the order of the statement is significant just because the assumption throughout the Gospel is that another hearing of Jesus' voice is not only possible but also actual. In the second chapter, for example, the Evangelist writes: "When [Jesus] was in Jerusalem during the Passover festival, many believed in his name because they saw the signs that he was doing. But Jesus on his part would not entrust himself to them for he himself knew what was in everyone" (2:23–25). According to the Evangelist, this wholly external kind of belief, based as it is on miracles instead of on inward assent to the truth and being of it existentially, is ultimately but a species of unbelief. In the final analysis, it does not really hear Jesus' voice because it is not of the truth.

I may remind you that this conception of the possibility of another inauthentic faith in Jesus is one of the major themes of the so-called First Letter of John, which, whether or not it was actually written by the author of the Fourth Gospel, certainly belongs to the same world of fundamental understanding. You'll recall, I'm sure, the many parallels in the Letter to a passage such as this: "Whoever says, 'I have come to know him,' but does not obey his commandments is a liar, and in such a person the truth does not exist; but whoever obeys his word, truly in this person the love of God has reached perfection. By this we may be sure that we are in him: whoever says, 'I abide in him,' ought to walk just as he walked" (1 John 2:4–6). This correlation of authentic faith in Jesus with obedience to his commandments—that is, with love of one another—also has many parallels in the "farewell discourses" of John's Gospel itself (chs. 13–17). As a matter of fact, throughout the Johannine writings, the acid test, so to speak, of what it means to be "in" Jesus or to "dwell" (or "abide") in him is just that "being of the truth," or that "doing what is true," that expresses itself in love. It's by no means accidental, then, that the First Letter so frequently addresses those who claim to be from God in terms of the imperative that they shall love their brothers and also, at the same time, boldly states that anyone who does thus love one's brothers (and, we would add, sisters) is born of God and knows God (4:7).

"Everyone who is of the truth hears my voice." This means, then, on the one hand, that everyone who, in the consciousness of one's own creatureliness and need before God, loves one's neighbors and ministers to their needs is already of the truth and is able to hear Jesus' voice and respond to his claim, if and when one ever actually hears it. On the other hand, Jesus' statement means that every claim to hear, or to have heard, his voice has to be tested by the extent to which the one who makes it actually does what is true, or as the First Letter puts it so beautifully, walks in the same way in which Jesus himself walked.

This interpretation is borne out, I think, by two things that emerge from considering the meaning of our text in its immediate context. There is, for one thing, the sentence preceding it in which the Evangelist has Jesus summarize the purpose of his work in the world in the words: "For this I was born, and for this I came into the world, to bear witness to the truth." Here, as in so many other places in the Gospel, the implication is clearly that even Jesus himself is subject to the authority of the truth to which he bears witness. In fact, one must say, I believe, that Jesus is who Christians assert him to be, the one who inaugurates the new, final era of reconciliation and salvation, precisely because of his subjection to the truth. There are, to be sure, many other similar statements in the Gospel, culminating in the great declaration of the fourteenth chapter that Jesus *is* the truth (14:6). And surely this is the final word that we as Christians are also bound to speak. Still, the really significant thing about Jesus' statement is that it's not some arbitrary claim, but rests, in the final analysis, upon the hard, unalterable, and stubborn fact that he really is the truth. Just as genuinely hearing his voice is not the purely external sort of belief that arises more out of a childish fascination with the extraordinary and miraculous than out of being existentially of the truth that is love, even so, his claim to be this truth is not based merely on some external and arbitrary power to enforce it but roots in the fact that he actually bears witness to, and in his own person mediates, that truth.

In saying this, however, we've already anticipated the other thing that's crucial to our understanding of the text—namely, that, as Jesus himself is made to affirm, his kingdom is not from this world. This familiar passage is not adequately interpreted if, as happens so often, one takes it to imply simply that the Christian faith is ultimately and irrelevantly otherworldly. Rather, as the context itself clearly shows, the point of the statement is that Jesus' authority, unlike that of Caesar and of the other rulers of the world, rests not on some external power to enforce it, but on the inescapable power of the truth itself. Even though his servants do not fight to keep him from falling into the hands of his enemies; even though he's judged and executed by nothing less than the power of imperial Rome, the Johannine Jesus is able to affirm with sublime confidence, "Now is the judgment of this world; now the ruler of this world will be driven out" (12:31). This juxtaposition of the overruling power of the truth with the arbitrary power of all the kingdoms of this world is the nerve of the so-called Johannine irony that defines the dramatic structure and movement of the entire Gospel; and, in the last analysis, it's what lies behind the fact that the sort of eschatology, or understanding of last things, that conceives of God as a kind of super-Caesar who will redress the inexact judgments of history on some unbelievable "last day" finds no place in the Gospel's way of thinking. The arbitrariness and externality of any such conception give way to the profound insight that "this is the judgment, that the light has come into the world, and people loved darkness rather than light because their deeds were evil" (3:19).

The abiding witness of the Fourth Gospel is that the truth has its way whether or no, and all the power of the world cannot keep the disgrace of a Roman cross from revealing the transcendent glory of God and of God's only Son to any who are willing to behold it. And the living word that our text would communicate to us, also, is that the knowledge of the only true God and of Jesus Christ whom he has sent, which itself is eternal life, can only be realized—but always is realized—by being of the truth that is love, and that, apart from such being, no claim to have heard the voice of the Son of God that bestows life can withstand the inexorable judgment that overcomes everyone who is not of the truth. Jesus is the truth! This is the message of our text to us; and it tells us not only that we do not really hear his voice unless we are of the truth that he is, but also that, whenever and wherever any of us is of that truth, there he is in the midst of us, and we are summoned to behold his glory.

II

But what does this message concretely mean for us? What does it have to say to our particular situation today?

For one thing, I think, it wants to say something to us about our shared responsibility as ministers and theologians, as those who, in our time and place, are charged with the preaching and teaching ministry of the Christian church, and also with thinking critically about its adequacy and fittingness. To those of us who either now are, or presently will be, responsible for preaching the gospel within the situation of the institutional church, it's a warning that our job is never done until we have succeeded in translating the meaning of Jesus who is the truth into terms that are both understandable and fitting to the concrete condition of those to whom we would speak. It tells us that we do well to preach less *about* Jesus and more *of* him, that is, of what the truth he is means for the particular situation of our hearers. Both because the classic Christian words and symbols have been so largely emptied of their meaning for many people and because there's a tendency toward abstractionism and irrelevance in all preaching and teaching that moves solely or even primarily within the realm of these classical symbols, it's impossible for any serious preacher or teacher today to avoid this difficult task of translation. In order to preach Jesus in our situation, we must seek, first of all and always, to preach the truth that he is; and this is a truth that, by its very nature, is at once eternally the same and forever different. It is ever the same, namely, insofar as it is love; but it is also always different, insofar as this love ever acquires partly new and different meanings depending on the necessities and opportunities of each new concrete situation. Within the limits of the freedom by which Jesus has made us free, and with a due sense of our own inadequacy and of the sovereign freedom of God, we must constantly struggle to spell out the meaning of the truth that Jesus is as it emerges out of the immediate situation in which we stand. This means, specifically, that we must continually concern ourselves with such things as defining "middle axioms" and developing a casuistry that is capable of applying the law of love through imperatives fitting to the particular needs of the present.

In all of this, of course, there's always the risk that we will confuse our truth with the truth that Jesus is. But our text tells us that this risk must be taken. It also tells us that the risk is lessened somewhat to the extent that we're serious in our attempts to discern the truth, instead of being concerned overmuch with being "relevant" by saying things that our contemporaries would like us to say. In any case, earnestly seeking the truth is already a way of being of it.

But our text doesn't just speak to us as ministers who have to preach and teach; it also wants to say something to us as theologians—and it especially wants to say something about the procedure we have to follow in our efforts to provide a solid theoretical foundation for the practical ministry of the church. It tells us, I believe, that our theology must be apologetic from first to last. By "apologetic" in this connection, I mean essentially what Paul Tillich meant when he said now almost two decades ago: "If there may be any apologetics today, this is the only way to perform it: not defense of Christianity and negation of its foes, but interpretation of them from the Christian point of view."

The notion that appears again and again to plague Protestant Christianity, that the world outside the church is an undifferentiated "mass of perdition," simply will not bear scrutiny. God has nowhere been left without witness, and, in ways beyond our knowing, women and men who have never heard the Christian gospel, or having heard it, have, in all conscience, declined to accept it have known God's "uncovenanted mercies" and, by reason of what Anglican theologians often refer to as the ministry of the "unincarnate Logos," have come to be of the truth that Jesus is. In the Marxist criticism of an effete bourgeois civilization and of a church that has become so ensconced in the status quo that it has forsaken the prophetic and reconciling ministry to which it's called, there's a truth that we as Christians can ignore only at the peril of not really hearing Jesus' voice. By the same token, the self-understanding that informs a thoroughly secular science that wants to look at things as they are and refuses to brook the arbitrary limits placed on human inquiry by an authoritarian church is not all that dissimilar to the self-understanding of Christian faith itself.

This point is confirmed, interestingly enough, by something William Lee Miller has written in an article on Reinhold Niebuhr that appeared in a recent issue of *The Reporter*: "In a way," Miller writes, "what Niebuhr does is to take our twentieth-century understanding of cultural relativism and apply it more thoroughly than its secular spokesmen. He takes the awareness of the need for self-criticism and self-correction, which comes partly from a modern scientific outlook, and applies it even to that outlook." In short, Miller concludes, "[Niebuhr] sees a central truth with which our age is concerned, the relativity of all positions; [and] he speaks for a central virtue which our time has recognized, self-criticism."

The creative cultural movements in our situation are, indeed, not unaware of the truth that the church exists to proclaim, although they may and do confuse it with their own truth and, like the rest of us, all too frequently betray it in their actions. But, as Tillich has said, theology cannot relate itself to such a situation by any simple strategy of defense and attack but, on the contrary, has to seek to interpret these various movements from the standpoint of Christian faith. It goes without saying that such an interpretation will be dialectical in character, in that it will involve not only affirmation of the truth in these movements, but also negation of the falsehood with which that truth is undoubtedly mixed. There's as much reason for us to pronounce the judgment of the cross against the false religions of our day as there was for the prophets, apostles, martyrs, and reformers who have preceded us. But we must constantly be on guard lest the word we preach be but some human word that will only further estrange our hearers from that Word who is the light and life of all humankind.

To treat the creative efforts at self-understanding that are current in the culture at large as merely so many attempts at sinful self-justification—or as expressing merely the question to which the Christian message alone can supply the answer—is to run the risk of confounding the kingdom of Jesus who is the truth with the kingdoms of this world. Unless the Christian faith speaks directly to the soul of everyone and calls one to acknowledge the truth that one can deny only by suppressing it and living inauthentically in bad faith, it can maintain itself only because of the inertia of its institutions or the pleasant but accidental associations its symbols may happen to evoke from the "collective unconscious."

It's one of the ironies of much of the so-called Neo-Protestantism of our time that, in its refusal to admit that the gospel is subject to a criterion of truth that, in the last analysis, is written on the heart of every one of God's children, it brings the kingdom of Jesus down to the level of the competing kingdoms of this world. When the acceptance or rejection of Christian faith is made to depend on a "decision" beyond which one cannot go and that can be tested only by abandoning it, then we've left the New Testament and the Reformation and have gone over to Greece and Rome. Our problem as human beings is not a problem of knowledge, and we don't need some unchallengeable authority to give us answers that we ourselves are powerless to obtain. What we do need is the ever-new reassurance that God does not lie and that the way of the cross, which in the depth of our being we always know we should follow, is the way to eternal life.

This is the truth that it is the business of the theology of our day, as of every other day, to see gets communicated to the world. And our text suggests that it is communicated best if we seek, first of all, to make contact with it as it finds expression in the honest attempts at self-understanding by the serious minds of our time. In the name of God the Father who has written this truth on all of our hearts and has redeemed us by its power decisively through Jesus the Son, we must speak the word of reassurance that will enable those of our generation to embrace it as the truth that in no way means death for them but only ever more abundant life.

Finally, our text would say something to us as those who not only must preach and teach the truth that Jesus is, but must also again and again allow it to be preached to us and allow ourselves to be taught by it. To those among us who are prone to be too confident that we've already heard Jesus's voice, it's a warning that, without that being of the truth—or, in the words of the Psalmist, "without that truth in the inward being" (Ps 51:6)—that is love, the voice we're hearing is not Jesus' at all, but only our own. And to any of us who sometimes despair of ever hearing Jesus' voice, it is a promise that, insofar as we submit all that we are to the overruling power of God's love and, in returning love, seek to meet the concrete needs of our neighbors, we need never fear of not hearing Jesus' voice. For his word abides: "Everyone who is of the truth hears my voice." Amen.

6 DECEMBER 1959

Luke 21:25–36

"There will be signs in the sun, the moon, and the stars, and on the earth distress among nations confused by the roaring of the sea and the waves. People will faint from fear and foreboding of what is coming upon the world, for the powers of the heavens will be shaken. Then they will see 'the Son of Man coming in a cloud' with power and great glory. Now when these things begin to take place, stand up and raise your heads, because your redemption is drawing near."

Then he told them a parable: "Look at the fig tree and all the trees; as soon as they sprout leaves you can see for yourselves and know that summer is already near. So also, when you see these things taking place, you know that the kingdom of God is near. Truly, I tell you, this generation will not pass away until all things have taken place. Heaven and earth will pass away, but my words will not pass away.

"Be on your guard so that your hearts are not weighed down with dissipation and drunkenness and the worries of this life, and that day catch you unexpectedly, like a trap. For it will come upon all who live on the face of the whole earth. Be alert at all times, praying that you may have the strength to escape all these things that will take place, and to stand before the Son of Man."

I

One of the great lessons in the church's lectionary is the Gospel appointed for today, the Second Sunday in Advent. For generations, the church has made use of this lesson to proclaim its message of the coming of God's reign of judgment and grace. Nor can there be any question that the church intends the lesson also for us. Its witness is addressed not only to this person or nation, but to all—and this means also to you and me.

There is a question, however, whether this lesson can any longer communicate the church's witness to us today. Intended for us it may be, but if we're to be confronted with the word it speaks, it must be a lesson that we can understand. Yet this is the very thing we cannot take for granted. Neither for us nor for our contemporaries generally is it at all self-evident that this lesson has anything to say to us at all. There's a twofold reason for this.

First, the lesson, like so much in the New Testament writings, assumes a mythological picture of the world. By "mythological" here I mean what is commonly understood by the term as it's used in the scientific, or critically reflective, study of religions—namely, a kind of outlook for which the realm of the transcendent, of the holy or the divine as well as the demonic, is pictured naively in the concepts and terms that properly apply only to the realm of the nondivine. So, for example, the mythological mind typically thinks of God as dwelling high in the sky, in a heavenly world only spatially distant from the world of ordinary events and experiences. Thus, in our lesson, Jesus pictures the Son of Man descending on the clouds of heaven with power and great glory and exhorts his hearers to look up and raise their heads when these events of the end-time begin to take place. Likewise, his statements that redemption (or the kingdom of God) is "drawing near" indicate that he thinks just as naively of the divine realm in terms of time as in terms of space. The future advent of God's kingdom is but one more event—although, of course, an extraordinary, miraculous one—in the midst of, and alongside, all the other events in the historical process.

Therefore, from the standpoint of the critical student of religions, what is reflected in our text is simply the mythological world-picture of late Jewish apocalyptic, which was so prominent a feature of the environment in which Christianity took its rise. With its expectation of the imminent end of the old age and its ample inventory of the stock features of apocalyptic fantasy, the passage is a typical instance of the mythological view of the world everywhere assumed in the earliest expressions of the Christian witness.

But, second, such a mythological view is bound to seem alien and incredible to us today. Largely as a result of the phenomenal growth of science and technology, which is arguably the most significant development in the modern history of the West, our thinking as been so determined that the mythological world-picture of the Christian tradition cannot but strike us as irrevocably passé. Nor is this true only of those of us who directly share in the ongoing processes of scientific research and are sophisticated about scientific thinking and procedure. Even ordinary persons, whose view of the world is increasingly determined by the achievements of a science-based technology, are unable to credit traditional mythological claims. They know as surely as the trained scientist how senseless it is to speak of "up" and "down" in the universe in which they live, and how impossible, accordingly, is the notion of a heavenly realm of the divine situated somewhere "above" the world of mundane occurrences. And if the astronomer, as Laplace said, has no need of the "God hypothesis" to account for the movement of the stars, ordinary persons have just as little need of it to make use of their electric shavers or their hair dryers, or any of the countless other appliances of our technological civilization.

Furthermore, women and men today cannot honestly look forward to the imminent or eventual end of the world and Christ's returning on the clouds of heaven to hold final judgment and to dispense supernatural salvation and damnation. They're accustomed to viewing the course of events as an immensely intricate natural process that follows its own orderly laws of change and development; and if they even think of the world's coming to an end, they take for granted that this, too, would be due entirely to natural and not supernatural causes or conditions.

To be sure, the dreaded prospect of thermonuclear annihilation has sometimes seemed to give the terrors of the apocalypse a meaning for us that they scarcely had earlier in our century. But anyone who thinks about it realizes that the destruction of our earth in a nuclear holocaust is something wholly other than an end of the world brought about by the intervention of divine or supernatural powers. And when confronted with Jesus' words that "this generation will not pass away until all things have taken place," contemporary women and men are bound to ask whether the refutation of this promise by two millennia of history isn't more than sufficient evidence of its falsity.

No one will question, of course, that there are exceptions to my generalization and that superstition in various forms continues to manifest itself on the edges of our scientific-technological civilization. Even so, the real exceptions are probably fewer than we might suppose were we to judge solely from what people profess to believe. Do we not often protest our assent to things that in fact have little or no bearing on the way we actually understand ourselves and lead our lives? And what of the different forms of superstition that we see? Don't they confirm my generalization rather than deny it? Aren't the credulous souls who consult the astrology pages in their newspapers in a very different position from the devout believers in astral religion who were so numerous a company in late antiquity?

Superstitious persons today stand on the periphery and not at the center of their civilization; and it is obvious—at times, surely, even to them—that they're fighting a losing battle. At any rate, those of us who are gathered here, like the vast majority of our contemporaries, cannot accept as our own the mythological picture of the world reflected in our lesson. Because we're the modern women and men we are, we have to ask not only what this lesson would say to us, but also whether it really has anything to say to us at all. Is there any way of interpreting it that will permit it to say all that it really intends to say, and yet do this so that we today who no longer think and speak mythologically can understand it as confronting us with a genuine possibility of decision?

II

There is a way of approaching our lesson that permits it to speak to us, and if we follow this way it will be discovered to have something to say to us that we will definitely be the better for having heard. In any event, it will be seen to offer us a possibility for understanding our lives and leading them that confronts us with a real choice. If we're unable to make this choice and to understand ourselves as it directs, it will no longer be because it asks us to believe an incredible mythology, but because we're unwilling to make the kind of personal decision about ourselves, about our own lives as human beings, that it summons us to make.

The key to the lesson's meaning is to recognize that the real purpose of its thinking and speaking as it does is only very imperfectly achieved by its language, by its concepts and terms. The intention of myth is to think and speak of the transcendent reality that we all experience as the ground and limit of our own existence and of the entire created order. But in thinking and speaking of this reality, myth so represents it that it seems to be just one more item, however extraordinary, in the cosmic whole. Thus myth appears as though its purpose is scientific instead of religious, as though it's simply another, more primitive way of knowing about the same reality that the various sciences are properly concerned to know. As a result, it seems to conflict with the sciences and to be marginalized by them when they fail to credit the claims it apparently makes.

But this well-known conflict completely obscures myth's real intention; and this is true even though the language of myth itself makes the conflict seem plausible and the defenders of myth are often tragically slow to recognize its real purpose. Myth does not really intend to speak about matters that are the proper concern of the special sciences, human as well as natural, but rather seeks to express our inalienable sense of dependence, and of the dependence of all things like us, upon an ultimate ground of being and meaning that is the ever-present primal source and final end of our lives and of all created things.

Thus the purpose of apocalyptic mythology in speaking, as it does, about the end of the world is not to provide a bizarre description of extraordinary phenomena, but rather to present an understanding of human life in its natural and historical context that is a perennial possibility for human choice. It wants to say that the final justification for our lives and for the whole created order is never to be found within ourselves or within that order, but solely in the grace and judgment of God that constantly impinge on us as our primal source and our final end. What alone endows our fleeting lives with abiding significance is that they make a real difference to something radically beyond themselves—not simply that they give rise to other created events that must also cry out for justification, but that the whole creative process at each of its stages and in all of its parts is assessed by a transcendent judgment and thereby rendered everlastingly significant.

Apart from such a transcendent judgment, for which nothing that happens is merely indifferent and which is able to preserve the present from slipping irrecoverably into the past, our creaturely lives would be utterly devoid of any lasting meaning. For mortals like us, the rule holds good that "in the midst of life we are in death." Nor is this merely the death that must one day bring each of our lives to its close. It is also that deeper death whereby every present accomplishment is "perpetually perishing."

Hardly have we grasped the present and made it ours than it slips away forever into the receding past. Our own poor powers of memory and judgment are unable to retain it in the living immediacy of each new present; and if it lingers with us at all, it is as but an ever-vanishing shade of its former reality.

Hence our deep human need to be accepted, to be known and cherished for exactly what we are, can never be met—never even begin to be met—merely by the judgments of our fellow human beings. Although we seek each other's approval, and may despair when we cannot find it, we're haunted by the knowledge that creatures as fallible and impermanent as ourselves cannot possibly supply the final judgment for which we yearn, the ultimate acceptance that can alone endow our lives with an abiding meaning.

It is of just such a final judgment, however, that apocalyptic mythology intends to speak. Its purpose is not to refer us to yet another, however incredible, happening in either the near or the remote future, but rather to point us to the transcendent love of God that embraces every happening as its primal source and final end. In this way, it summons us to a new understanding and living of our lives. It tells us that we both can and should understand ourselves in the light of God's all-embracing love and so realize the inner freedom from our past and for our future that that love alone makes possible.

When our lesson, then, speaks of the dramatic events that will signal the end of the present, old age and the imminent coming of the Son of Man to bring in the future, new age, with its final judgment and redemption, it's really speaking of the two most insistent realities of our human condition in every moment of our lives. It reminds us, first, that, in the world in which we live, nothing whatever is fixed and permanent. So far as we can see, our lives and the whole created order to which we belong, are constantly slipping into what, for us, is the nothingness of the past. And when it speaks of "distress among nations" and says that "people will faint from fear and foreboding of what is coming upon the world," it but expresses our anxiety whenever this transience, this perpetual perishing, of every creaturely present, suddenly overwhelms us.

But it's in just this situation of anxiety, it says, that our redemption is "drawing near." The point is not just that God is now closer to us because we're anxious, or that the cracks in things more clearly reveal God's presence than things themselves. Rather, it's the same point expressed in the old saying that "our extremity is God's opportunity." Just when we're overtaken by the perpetual perishing of all our good and by our utter helplessness to secure for our lives any lasting meaning, we may be led to look up and raise our heads so as to receive the security of God's grace. In this sense, the passing away of the present order and the shaking of even the powers of the heavens are "signs" of God's approaching redemption. As surely as the leafing of the trees is followed by the coming of summer, so surely are the transient events of our lives followed by the advent of God's everlasting kingdom.

And most important: all this is happening now—in every now! "Truly, I tell you, this generation will not pass away"—will not slip forever from the immediacy of the present—"until all things have taken place"—until all things are completely known and all forgiven in the loving judgment of God. The final end of every present, of this very moment now, is to be received into the everlasting kingdom of God's love, there to be known and cherished forever for exactly what it is. What for us constantly slips into the irrecoverable past is for God preserved in an eternal present from which nothing can evermore be lost. And this eternal present of God's love, of God's judgment and grace, is even now our final end, the ultimate context in which all our lives are set.

Thus our text summons us to a new understanding of ourselves. Because the final truth about us is that even now we're all freely received by God's love, we're both enabled and commanded to be free from our past, from what we already are, and open for our future, for what we can and should become. We need not and ought not to be burdened by the cares of this life, by the anxious striving to secure our existence in a perpetually perishing world. It's just when we lose ourselves in the things of the world by trying to find in them a meaning for our lives that we fall subject to their power and to the power of death. Then it is that the inevitable transience of everything creaturely can suddenly entrap us. When we set our hearts too completely on the ever-perishing goods of the present age and fail to remember the final shadow under which they all stand, we but make ourselves vulnerable to their inevitable passing away.

Therefore, our lesson admonishes us to be watchful at all times and to pray for the strength to escape from the fate of every created thing. It is not that we're to ask to be relieved from the necessity of dying, much less to be gathered to some heavenly realm where this necessity supposedly no longer exists. The fact is sure that both "heaven and earth will pass away," and that heaven will pass away no less completely than earth. No, the only strength for which we're to pray is the strength that comes from

God's unbegun and unending love; and the only escape we're to seek is the escape that this love alone can and does provide.

But with this strength we may also hope to stand before the Son of Man. In being freed from our past and the anxious care that binds us to it, we can and should be open to meet the needs of our neighbors as ourselves. And, as we're taught by another word in the New Testament, to realize this possibility and to fulfill this demand is precisely what it means to stand in the day of the Lord's appearing. "Then the king will say to those at his right hand, 'Come, you that are blessed by my Father, inherit the kingdom prepared for you from the foundation of the world; for . . . just as you did it to one of the least of these who are members of my family, you did it to me'" (Matt 25:34-40). In every encounter with our neighbors in which we're open to meet their needs as our own, we receive nothing other or less than the final benediction of the Lord Jesus himself; and in that day when he shall come in all his glory—which is to say, in the very moment of our present encounter with our neighbors—we shall surely be caused to stand.

This is the meaning that our lesson has for us. And when we so interpret it, it teaches us to understand not only the significance of the season of Advent, but also the innermost meaning of the Christian witness itself. For to live as a Christian means to have just this understanding of one's life: to look forward to the imminent coming of God's kingdom and thereby to be freed from one's past and open for the future, with its gift and demand.

Of course, Christians look forward to this coming kingdom on the strength of a word that has already come to them through the life and death of Jesus Christ. But this word already spoken is a promise in time redeemed only in eternity. The kingdom of God to which it points is a kingdom that is always coming and only in this sense a kingdom that has already come. It impinges on every moment as its final end, and so is eternally present. But it is never present so that it may be simply identified with some particular happening or stage in the temporal order. Rather, as the decisive event of God's grace and judgment, it is also always beyond the world and is also eternally future.

This is why the Christian life is no merely static thing that may be settled once and for all by an act of intellectual assent to certain beliefs. It is not primarily a matter of beliefs at all, whether mythological or not, but is, first and last, a matter of each one of us understanding one's own personal life, which must be constantly settled anew by one's concrete decision in the moment.

May God give us the grace to make this decision and to keep ourselves open for the coming of God's kingdom all our lives through. For the promise of our text is sure: "This generation will not pass away until all things have taken place. Heaven and earth will pass away, but my words will not pass away." Amen.

6 April 1960

John 13:1–17, 20

Now before the festival of the Passover, Jesus knew that his hour had come to depart from this world and go to the Father. Having loved his own who were in the world, he loved them to the end. The devil had already put it into the heart of Judas son of Simon Iscariot to betray him. And during supper Jesus, knowing that the Father had given all things into his hands, and that he had come from God and was going to God, got up from the table, took off his outer robe, and tied a towel around himself. Then he poured water into a basin and began to wash the disciples' feet and to wipe them with the towel that was tied around him. He came to Simon Peter, who said to him, "Lord, are you going to wash my feet?" Jesus answered, "You do not know now what I am doing, but later you will understand." Peter said to him, "You will never wash my feet." Jesus answered, "Unless I wash you, you have no share with me." Simon Peter said to him, "Lord, not my feet only but also my hands and my head!" Jesus said to him, "One who has bathed does not need to wash, except for the feet, but is entirely clean. And you are clean, though not all of you." For he knew who was to betray him; for this reason he said, "Not all of you are clean."

After he had washed their feet, had put on his robe, and had returned to the table, he said to them, "Do you know what I have done to you? You call me Teacher and Lord—and you are right, for that is what I am. So if I, your Lord and Teacher, have washed your feet, you also ought to wash one another's feet. For I have set you an example, that you also should do as I have done to you. Very truly, I tell you, servants are not greater than their master, nor are messengers greater than the one who sent them. If you know these

18

*things, you are blessed if you do them . . . Very truly, I tell you, who-
ever receives one whom I send receives me; and whoever receives me
receives him who sent me."*

You'll have recognized that our lesson consists of two main parts. First,
there is the poignant portrayal of Jesus' washing the disciples' feet, together with an interpretation of his act developed through Simon Peter's
question and statements and Jesus' statements in reply. Then, second,
there is the other and somewhat different interpretation of the act that
Jesus gives himself after he has once again put on his garments and re-
sumed his place at the table.

The problem of interpreting the lesson, and thus of hearing the
word that it would also speak to us, lies in understanding these two parts
and rightly grasping their two interpretations of Jesus' action. Let's look
somewhat more closely, then, to see if we can understand the meaning
of our lesson.

We may note, first, that the concrete act of washing the disciples'
feet is clearly intended by the Evangelist to whom we owe our lesson to be
a symbol of something other than itself. This is not only suggested by the
obviously symbolic character of Jesus' acts throughout John's Gospel, but
it is also stated explicitly later in chapter 15, when Jesus is represented as
saying to the disciples, "You have already been cleansed by the word that
I have spoken to you" (v. 3). There can be no question that Jesus' washing
the disciples' feet is completely misunderstood if it's taken as anything
other than a symbolic representation of his whole ministry as God's word
to humankind. What John does is to set forth in a highly dramatic way
the single act of God's speaking to women and men decisively through
the humble form of the man Jesus of Nazareth.

If this is so, then the exchange with Peter through which the meaning of Jesus' act is more fully explained also needs to be understood differently than we might be inclined to understand it. The point of Peter's
refusing to let Jesus wash his feet is not simply that he refuses an act of
human kindness. What would be his motive for refusing such an act? No,
the point of his refusal is that, like all human beings, even those who belong to the community of the disciples, he is not willing to acknowledge
the presence of God in the lowly form of a human ministry. This, at any
rate, is the only way to make sense of his refusal if Jesus' action has the
symbolic meaning I have suggested. What is portrayed in Peter's initial
response to Jesus' offer to wash his feet is humankind's all but instinctive

turning away from the scandal of an actual meeting with the holy God. So long as God is merely an idea in our minds or removed from our life by being imagined enthroned in some remote and otherworldly heaven, we cannot but refuse God's ministry to us through the concrete happenings of life itself. By the same token, the decisive test of our openness to God as God really is is not whether we can talk about God either in eloquent words of wisdom or in critical theological reflections on them. Rather, it is whether we can faithfully receive God's ministry to us as and when it meets us here and now through merely human words and deeds of witness.

This is to say that the warning of Jesus to Peter is also addressed to us. "Unless I wash you, you have no share with me." Unless we're willing to receive God's ministry as it's offered to us through Jesus we cannot participate in the salvation he would bestow.

But the interesting thing about our lesson is that Peter's first response is not his last. As soon as he hears Jesus' warning, he makes a complete about-face and goes to the other extreme: "Lord, not my feet only, but also my hands and my head!" Yet this second response also meets with Jesus' disapproval. "One who has bathed does not need to wash, except for the feet, but is entirely clean. And you are clean." Jesus wants to be clear, in other words, that there is a false as well as a true way of hearing his warning. If we have no part in God's salvation unless we're willing to receive it in an actual meeting with Jesus, such receiving is completely misunderstood if it is thought of in merely quantitative terms. What is required is not simply a quantity of encounters with Jesus, but rather the kind or quality of encounter with him through which he can do his work in us and so cleanse us from all uncleanness. The one thing needful is not that we shall endlessly expose ourselves to Jesus' life and teachings, but that we shall faithfully hear the word that he speaks and is and that alone is sufficient to cleanse us from all our sin. Once this encounter has taken place, once we've heard the word of God's acceptance in spite of our being unacceptable, we are clean all over and need not wash again.

But this statement, too, is easily misunderstood. And so Jesus immediately adds, "though not all of you are clean." Even those within the community of the disciples who have in some sense already been made clean by his word are not safe from the danger of once again falling away. The reason for this lies in the very nature of faith itself. Just because faith is in no sense something quantitative, it is also impossible to think of it as a once-for-all decision that, having once been made, relieves a disciple of ever having to make it again. If faith is completely different from a sheer quantity of encounters with Jesus, it is also different from a single act in which we give assent to Christian "beliefs" or affiliate ourselves with the Christian church. Indeed, faith is nothing other than the constantly renewed personal decision to receive for oneself in each new present God's ministry to us decisively through Jesus. What is conveyed to us through Jesus' prophecy of Judas' betrayal is this understanding of the nature of faith. It reminds us that the only way in which we can rightly hear the word, "and you are clean," is by appropriating it to ourselves through a renewed decision of faith.

What is presented, then, in the first part of our lesson is the twofold foundation of our life in the Christian community: there is, first, the always prevenient act of God's grace, which is made known to us decisively through Jesus; and there is, second, our own personal decision of faith, through which alone we are able to receive God's grace so as to realize its cleansing power.

But if this is the meaning of the first part of our lesson, it leaves us with a question. If what it means to be a Christian is to receive Jesus' ministry to us through obedient faith, how can we today satisfy this condition? How can we each appropriate for ourselves the ministry of a man who lived some two millennia ago and with whom we can no longer have any immediate association?

We get an answer to this question, I think, in the second part of our lesson, where, you'll remember, Jesus is made to give yet another interpretation of his symbolic act of washing the disciples' feet. Here the emphasis falls on the significance of his act as an example, which the disciples are summoned to imitate. "You call me Teacher and Lord," Jesus says, "and you are right, for that is what I am. So if I, your Lord and Teacher, have washed your feet, you also ought to wash one another's feet. For I have set you an example, that you also should do as I have done to you."

But if what is signified by Jesus' own act is his ministry as God's word, then it is only logical to suppose that his summons to the disciples to imitate his act is in reality a call to them to continue his ministry of bearing witness. And this supposition is completely confirmed by the statement that follows: "Very truly, I tell you, servants are not greater than their master, nor are messengers greater than the one who sent them." By speaking of his disciples as messengers who are sent, Jesus makes clear that it is to the prophetic ministry of bearing witness that he is in reality commissioning the community when he calls them to imitate his action. As he himself has been sent by the Father to minister to them, so he in turn sends them to witness to one another—and, as a statement in a later chapter makes clear, also to witness to "the world" (cf. 17:18).

But this evidently suggests an answer to our question. It is through the witness of the community that the foundational witness of Jesus himself ever continues to take place. "Very truly, I tell you, whoever receives one whom I send receives me; and whoever receives me receives him who sent me." What makes it possible for us today to have a part in Jesus' own cleansing ministry is the witness or message of the Christian church, through its preaching and its sacraments. But—and this is the point of the second part of our lesson—for one rightly to receive this ministry requires one to take upon oneself the responsibility of continuing it by also bearing witness: the witness through which Jesus himself continues to speak to every new present his word of judgment and grace.

The word, then, that speaks to us through our lesson at once points us to the foundation of our life in the Christian community and also reminds us of the outward forms that this life must invariably take. It tells us that to be a Christian means to hear in faith the word of God's grace addressed to us through the preaching and sacraments of the church and, following the example of the Lord whom it proclaims, to carry on in our present the same word and ministry of reconciliation.

O Lord Jesus, who stands in our midst even now, make the words and deeds of this hour fit vessels of your redeeming grace. Help us so to hear the word that you speak and are that we are cleansed by its power and may fitly proclaim it to one another and to the world. Amen.

17 May 1964

Luke 11:9–13

> *"So I say to you, Ask, and it will be given you; search, and you will find, knock, and the door will be opened for you. For everyone who asks receives, and everyone who searches finds, and for everyone who knocks, the door will be opened. Is there anyone among you who, if your child asks for a fish, will give a snake instead of a fish? Or if the child asks for an egg, will give a scorpion? If you then, who are evil, know how to give good gifts to your children, how much more will the heavenly Father give the Holy Spirit to those who ask him!"*

To the careful student of this text one thing about it immediately catches the eye. Except for some trivial details, it's an almost perfect parallel to another passage found in the Gospel according to Matthew (7:7–11).

I say almost perfect parallel because there's one important difference between the two passages that stands out all the more sharply because they're otherwise so much alike. In Matthew's version—which is certainly the older—the concluding sentence reads as follows: "If you then, who are evil, know how to give good gifts to your children, how much more will your Father in heaven give good things to those who ask him?" Luke, by contrast, replaces the words "good things" with the words "the Holy Spirit," thereby giving the whole text a rather different appearance than it has in Matthew. The content of the promise, "Ask, and it will be given you" is no longer defined by the wholly general term "good things," but is understood to be the quite specific gift by God of God's own personal presence and power as the Holy Spirit.

Except for this difference, of course, the church would never have selected our text—even as late as it did—as a proper lesson for this Sunday,
the feast of Pentecost. But this suggests that a likely way to understand
what the text would teach us is to reflect together on the significance of
this difference. What's the point when the gift it promises simply for the
asking is not the plural gift of "good things," but the singular gift of God's
own Holy Spirit?

Maybe if we can answer this question, we'll be in a position to hear
the word our text addresses to us. And then perhaps we can also listen
in a new way to that other lesson read earlier (John 14:15–31), through
which the church has traditionally proclaimed the Spirit's coming at Pentecost and the meaning of that event for us all.

I

We may begin with some obvious comments on the text in the more
familiar setting given it by Matthew. You will agree, I think, that its opening sentences, when read in this setting, give ample cause for offense to
anyone with even a modicum of critical judgment. When we're told that
"everyone who asks receives, and everyone who searches finds, and for
everyone who knocks, the door will be opened," our response is apt to
be as incredulous as when we hear those other words from Matthew's
Gospel, "all who take the sword will perish by the sword" (26:52). Many
an old soldier does not die by the sword, but simply fades away; and it's
just as evident that wishing does not make it so. The gap, sometimes the
unbridgeable gap, between what we ask for and what we receive—isn't it
one of the facts of life of which we have each learned more than enough
in the hard school of experience? And how many are the doors on which
we have knocked again and again only to have them remain as firmly
closed to us as ever? A full century after we fought the costliest war in our
history to redeem the promise of our founding as a free nation, millions
of our fellow citizens are still barred from entering fully on the rights
thereby won for them—and that in spite of all the knocking on the doors
of the intervening years.

True, it's just by presupposing such a situation to be possible among
us that the text seeks to make its point. It takes for granted that human
beings are evil and therefore, for the most part, insensitive to the claims
of their needy neighbors. So it argues from the lesser to the greater and

tries to show that God responds to the petitions of God's children with a goodness that is at best adumbrated by the occasional kindnesses of sinful women and men. But surely the pleas of Negroes for the equal justice still denied them have not been addressed solely to those human councils that have been so slow to hear them, much less to grant them. Have they not also lifted up their voices again and again to the God of their fathers, the God of Abraham, Isaac, and Jacob, who once brought Israel out of bondage into the land of promise? And what of the unanswered prayers of those hundreds of thousands who were herded to their slaughter like sheep in the unimaginable hell of Auschwitz? Were their petitions for mercy and human kindness directed merely to those who drove them to their death or passively witnessed it—or also to the One whose loving kindness had to endure the incalculable burden of their pain and suffering?

Christians have usually recognized, of course, that the question of unanswered prayer has its subtleties. Knowing that we're sinful human beings who do not know how to pray as we ought, they have been open to the witness classically expressed in the words of an unknown Confederate soldier:

> I asked God for strength, that I might achieve—
> I was made weak, that I might learn humbly to obey.
> I asked for health, that I might do greater things—
> I was given infirmity, that I might do better things.
> I asked for riches, that I might be happy—
> I was given poverty that I might be wise.
> I asked for power, that I might have the praise of men—
> I was given weakness, that I might feel the need of God.
> I asked for all things, that I might enjoy life—
> I was given life that I might enjoy all things.
> I got nothing I asked for—but everything I had hoped for.
> Almost despite myself, my unspoken prayers were answered.
> I among all men, most richly blessed!

And yet, whatever the truth of these words—and what believer would deny their truth?—they do not remove the stumbling block of Matthew's version of our text. On the contrary, they fully confirm it. "I got nothing I asked for," the soldier admits. And that's just the point: so long as the content of the promise is designated by the utterly general and indefinite term "good things," it's simply not true that "everyone who asks receives," nor can we credit the claim, "Ask and it will be given you." So far as the good things of this life are concerned, the gap between what we ask for and what we get can never be fully closed. The plain truth of the matter is that some human beings ask for a fish only to be given a snake, and for far too many the crushing burden of an unasked for and undeserved destiny seems all but to exclude the possibility of an honest faith in God.

Thus we're reminded once again of the great temptation of all religion to pretend to certainty about more things than it should and to make promises that it has no right to make. As Matthew presents them (however unintentionally), the words "Ask, and it will be given you" are an overextension of Christian confidence. It's scarcely surprising, then, that, for many of us, they're more of an obstacle to faith than a convincing summons to it.

II

But what of our text itself in the quite different setting given these words by Luke? Is it, too, open to this criticism?

Well, hardly. By changing Matthew's "good things" to the words "the Holy Spirit," Luke both avoids the difficulties that Matthew's version of the text raises and, at the same time, gives testimony to the unshakable confidence of Christian faith.

I mentioned a moment ago religion's perennial tendency to overextend the confidence proper to it by sometimes making claims that experience fails to justify. But this tendency is simply one particular expression of a deeper dilemma by which the whole of the religious life is threatened. If we're to think and speak of the Divine at all, it can only be by means of some kind of an analogy with the nondivine realities of our experience. As the Transcendent, or "wholly other," in the strict sense of the word, God cannot become much more for us than an ineffable presence unless we in some way bring God within the limits of our ordinary thought and speech. Either we must stand before God in virtual silence or else seek somehow to apprehend God in the same terms in which we must apprehend whatever it is given us to know.

And yet the great problem is that, in resolving this dilemma by choosing the second possibility, we only too easily forget the peculiar character of our religious thought and language. Concepts and words that can really be used only symbolically are continually misunderstood as having a straightforward literal meaning, with the result that God's radical otherness from us and our world is more or less seriously obscured. This difficulty is compounded, then, by our universal proclivity to understand ourselves—or, really, to *misunderstand* ourselves—in terms of what we are able to know and control, of what we objectively are and have and do. Instead of recognizing that the true meaning of our lives can only become real to us again and again anew through the honesty and integrity of our own personal decisions, we lose ourselves in the world of nondivine realities and try to secure a meaningful existence by the good things with which it presents us. Health, wealth, reputation, and success become for us the indispensable supports of the only life that's worth living.

It is this situation, implicit in the very nature of the religious life, that prompts the claim, "Christian faith is the end of religion." This claim does not mean that Christians somehow manage to think and speak of God otherwise than in the same symbolic way of human beings generally. Nor does it imply that they succeed where others fail in avoiding the fateful confusion of God's essential gift and demand with the various good things to which we all mistakenly look for the ultimate meaning of our life. The point, rather, is that wherever Christians are true to the faith that unites them, they preserve an acute sense of the radical otherness of God and refuse to domesticate God within the severe limits of their own knowledge and appreciation.

No one has seen this more clearly, I venture to think, than the great American iconoclast, H. L. Mencken.

> It is only the savage [he once wrote], whether of the African bush or the American gospel tent, who pretends to know the will and intent of God exactly and completely. 'For who hath known the mind of the Lord?' asked Paul of the Romans. 'How unsearchable are His judgments, and His ways past finding out!' 'It is the glory of God,' said Solomon, 'to conceal a thing.' 'Clouds and darkness,' said David, 'are around Him.' 'No man,' said the Preacher, 'can find out the work of God.' . . . The difference between religions is a difference in their relative content of agnosticism. The most satisfying and ecstatic faith is almost purely agnostic. It trusts absolutely without professing to know it all.

Christians realize that what's chiefly wrong with literalism in religious belief is not just that it's hard pressed by an ever-advancing science, but that it robs God of the majesty that belongs to God. And more important, they know that God's primary gift and demand to human beings is never simply the good things in themselves and their world that they can possess and dispose of, but God's own personal presence and power—God's own wholly free and all-embracing love, in which all the good things of life and life itself have their sole primal source and sole final end.

The genius of Christian faith, in short, is that it lets God really be God. It breaks through the innocent and not so innocent idolatries of our natural religion and witnesses to us that the final meaning of our life is never to be found in that life itself or in any mere extension of it. Rather, faith claims that this meaning is solely the gift of God's love—in fact, is that love itself—and so is infinitely, qualitatively different from ourselves and our world.

But one of the implications of this claim—indeed, I should say its chief implication—is that the fact of that gift, the fact of its having always already been given to each and every one of us, is absolutely certain. Just because the final meaning of our life is not this good thing or that, but God's own very being as love, it is the one thing of which we may each be completely confident. For what makes God God, what radically distinguishes God from literally everything else, is that God is under all conditions bound to be and always to be God. Whatever other things may be or not be, God can never fail to be; and it is from the depths of God's unfathomable love that these other things all proceed, even as it is to this love that they all at last return. So the great and final fact that the church speaks of as "redemption" is not merely one more particular fact besides the many others and continuous with them. It is, instead, the universal fact of God's never-failing love, in which all the other particular facts are embraced, and which is the ultimate ground of their significance.

Just this, I believe, is the point of our text. It can assure us, "Ask, and it will be given you," because the gift it promises us is not simply "good things," but "the Holy Spirit"—which is to say, God Godself, God's pure unbounded love, as personally and powerfully present in our own lives. Here, in this one unique case, the gap that otherwise obtains between what we ask for and what we're given simply cannot obtain, and the rule admits of no exceptions that "everyone who asks receives, and everyone who searches finds, and for everyone who knocks, the door will be opened."

This rule, in other words, is just like those other promises that are so familiar to us from the gospels: "All who exalt themselves will be humbled, but all who humble themselves will be exalted" (Luke 18:14; cf. 14:11 and Matt 23:12). Or "Those who try to make their life secure will lose it, but those who lose their life will keep it" (Luke 17:33; cf., e.g., Matt 10:39). These promises, too, are always open to misunderstanding, and unless we see them in their proper setting, it's easy enough to dismiss them. Nothing is more obvious in our day-to-day world, where we compete with one another for the good things of life, than that ambitious persons who exalt themselves are just those who get ahead, while humble persons are all too likely to get trampled in the rush.

But the whole point, of course, is that it is not of this world that these promises speak. On the contrary, they speak to us of the utterly different reality of God and of our relation to God, and, in *that* relation, they can never fail to be fulfilled. Here, in this one unique relationship, to exalt oneself is by that very fact to be humbled, and to seek to gain one's life is already to have lost it. By the very act through which we try to secure our existence by what we ourselves are and have and do, we're not only deceived as to our true condition, but are delivered into the hands of death, of that nothingness by which both we and our world are ever threatened. Henceforth the transitoriness of our life is no longer something merely natural, as provisional as life itself, but rather becomes for us the final power determining our destiny. Truly, for us, "Time is the tooth that gnaws. . . . we are born only to die and every day brings us one day nearer death" (John Dewey).

But the other half of the promises is no less sure of fulfillment. Just when we're willing to lose ourselves by humbly surrendering all our self-contrived securities, we can honestly acknowledge our actual condition, and God instead of death becomes for us the ultimate and determining power. Because nothing can be more certain than God's love for us, to turn away from ourselves and our own transitoriness is in that very moment to be exalted beyond death into God's eternal presence and to receive our life as a gift from God's hands. As one of the mystics has put it unforgettably, "To await God is to possess God."

And so, too, with the promise of our text. It would proclaim to us faith's one great certainty of God's unending love and bid each of us so to ask for that love that we may really receive it. This asking, of course, cannot be only or primarily a matter of words, or even of fully conscious thoughts. The real prayer is never something merely verbal or reflective, but is the more elemental petition that we are ourselves in our actual lives. To ask our heavenly Father for the Holy Spirit is to be open in our very existing to the presence and power of God's love as our only final security. It is to acknowledge honestly and with integrity our own limitations and to be ready for the ever-fresh encounters with our neighbors and our destiny through which both we and the world of our experience are continually transformed and made new.

And equally important to recognize is that our asking is in no way the condition of the Spirit's being given to us, but only of our receiving the gift. Here, above all, we must be mindful of the symbolic character of all our religious language and not be betrayed into a false literalism. The whole point of our text is to let God appear in God's majesty as God and to confront us with our possibility of new and authentic life. But we would miss the point completely if we supposed that God chooses to become God for us only because we open ourselves to God's presence and power. The only cause of God's love for us is God's love itself, and God's decision that we shall be God's people is always already prior to our decision that God shall be our God. Therefore, in asking for the Holy Spirit by opening our lives to God's presence, we do not initiate our relationship with God but only ratify it. We simply make fully our own the relation that God never fails to establish by embracing each and every one of us in God's unbounded love.

Were it otherwise, the promise of our text would once again be made uncertain, and there at least could be a gap between our asking and our receiving. But the teaching of the text is clear, and it excludes all such uncertainty. "Ask, and it will be given you. . . . For everyone who asks receives."

III

Yet surely *this* coming of the Spirit, which is promised to everyone who asks for it, is something different from the event the church remembers on this Pentecost Sunday. If we've rightly understood our text, its promise is universal. It witnesses to the reality of God's world-embracing love, and so to the possibility of God's becoming present in power as the Holy Spirit to anyone who is willing to receive God. In our New Testament lesson, on the other hand, the emphasis, at least, seems to lie elsewhere. There the descent of the Spirit is represented as a quite particular event of the historical past, and our reception of the Spirit is made to depend on our keeping a specific word and commandments that are also given historically. Thus Jesus says, in the words read from the Gospel according to John, "If you love me, you will keep my commandments. And I will ask the Father, and he will give you another Advocate, to be with you forever. This is the Spirit of truth" (14:15–17). Isn't the event foretold here something wholly different from the universal coming of the Spirit promised in our text? And isn't this event the real event of Pentecost?

If I decline simply to answer yes to these questions, it's not because I regard them as out of place. There is a difference here, and no one could deny that the event the church remembers at Pentecost is the decisive event of its own coming into being as the Christian church. And yet everything turns on rightly understanding this difference and on permitting this event to speak its own authentic word to us. My conviction is that our text and our lesson properly belong together and that they both acquire a new and deeper meaning when we listen to each of them in terms of the other.

When we hear our lesson in terms of the universal promise of our text, we're saved from a false understanding of the particular event in history whose meaning our lesson proclaims. We're enabled to see that the significance of Jesus Christ is not that, in him, God's Holy Spirit descends upon human beings for the first time, but that, through him, God's universal outpouring of the Holy Spirit has been promised to us explicitly and decisively and that this promise has met with the faith of a believing community. Even in our ordinary relationships with one another, we recognize that a gift is fully given, really becomes a gift, only when it is received. In this sense, faith affirms that it is through the event of Jesus Christ as known and proclaimed in the church that the gift of the Holy Spirit is fully given. Through this event, God's universal offer of God's love is actually received through a human word of promise having the same universal scope as that offer itself. "Ask, and it will be given you . . . For everyone who asks receives." It is this human word of promise, this completely universal word, that Jesus who is the Christ both speaks and is. And it is because this is so that, as Whitehead once put it, "the history of the world divides at this point."

But as surely as the meaning of our lesson is deepened by our text, it also deepens the text's meaning. It makes still clearer just how we're to understand the asking that the text represents as the only condition for receiving the gift of the Spirit. "If you would receive the Spirit of truth,"

Jesus tells the disciples, "then you must love me"—and that means, you must keep my commandments, or, as he also says, "You must keep my word." But what commandments, what word? Well, obviously, that of which Jesus is made to speak elsewhere in the same context in John's Gospel. "This is my commandment, that you love one another as I have loved you" (15:12; cf. 13:34).

Our lesson teaches us, in short, that the real test of our asking for God's Spirit is whether or not we're open in love to the concrete gift and demand of our fellow human beings. If we're really ready for the Spirit, willing to live solely by the security of God's love, then the proof of such willingness is our openness to our neighbors, our readiness to hear their pleas for justice and human kindness, and to act so that God's love for them is shown forth concretely. This does not mean, naturally, that it's because we thus keep Jesus's commandments that the gift of the Spirit is offered to us. No, in our lesson, as in our text, the assumption is clear that the offer of this gift has no other cause than God's own prior love for us as it is disclosed to us explicitly and decisively through Jesus. But it is solely where there is the earnest asking for this gift, and thus also the love of the neighbor that, knowingly or unknowingly, keeps Jesus' commandment, that the offer of the Spirit is actually received.

What is the word, then, that our text and our lesson together would say to us this Pentecost Sunday? It is, I believe, the same word proclaimed with beautiful simplicity by the German writer Ricarda Huch in her witness to the meaning of the Christian faith: "One who has not acknowledged the togetherness of human beings also has not acknowledged God, from whom all human beings proceed and to whom they return. . . . One who loves human beings is faithful and a child of God, even if one does not know it, yes, with words denies it. But one who does not love human beings is unfaithful, even were one to spend one's entire life in contemplating God and observing divine commandments."

The asking for the Spirit to which our text summons us is not some special religious exercise, whether contemplative fight or cultic observance, but that radical openness to God's love in our actual existence that proves itself unmistakably by our own love and concern for others as ourselves. Wherever we actually ask in this way, there occurs the real event of Pentecost, the real reception of God's gift of the Holy Spirit—and this event occurs whether we stand within the church, through whose word the gift of the Spirit is decisively promised to us, or whether we stand only within that far larger community whose boundaries no human being is given to discern. Amen.

John 6:5–14

When he looked up and saw a large crowd coming toward him, Jesus said to Philip, "Where are we to buy bread for these people to eat?" He said this to test him, for he himself knew what he was going to do. Philip answered him: "Six months' wages would not buy enough bread for each of them to get a little." One of his disciples, Andrew, Simon Peter's brother, said to him, "There is a boy here who has five barley loaves and two fish. But what are they among so many people?" Jesus said, "Make the people sit down." Now there was a great deal of grass in the place; so they sat down, about five thousand in all. Then Jesus took the loaves, and when he had given thanks, he distributed them to those who were seated; so also the fish, as much as they wanted. When they were satisfied, he told his disciples, "Gather up the fragments left over, so that nothing may be lost." So they gathered them up, and from the fragments of the five barley loaves, left by those who had eaten, they filled twelve baskets. When the people saw the sign that he had done, they began to say, "This is indeed the prophet who is to come into the world."

It was only after I'd already decided on what I would do in my sermon today that I suddenly realized the date would be 22 November. At first, I thought I'd simply go ahead with my plans and take no notice of the event that's surely in all our minds this Sunday morning. This was the easier to do because, frankly, I didn't want to take the time to prepare another sermon.

And yet the more I tried to go through with it, the clearer it became to me that it just wouldn't work. I was already suffering from a guilty conscience because the sermon I'd planned to use was one I'd prepared some months before, for a quite different occasion. For years, I've generally followed the practice of basing my sermons on the Propers of the Christian year as given in the Book of Common Prayer, and to us Methodists, in The Sunday Service prepared by Mr. Wesley. But this time, under the pressure of other duties, I'd resolved to suspend this discipline, hoping somehow to fit the meaning of this Sunday of the church year to the sermon I'd already worked out some time ago. And I would probably have gotten by with it if I hadn't had the lingering desire somehow to take into account what our church's tradition has taught on this particular day. For the turning point in the whole business came when I read the Gospel appointed for this Sunday, which we heard earlier as our New Testament lesson. All of a sudden, I knew my original plans would have to be scrapped and that it was to this Sunday that I would have to fit my sermon, instead of the other way around. This Sunday—the Sunday next before Advent and, by an accident of the calendar, also the first anniversary of 22 November 1963—this Sunday would somehow have to determine my words to you this morning.

Since that moment of sudden insight, it's become even clearer to me that these two elements in the meaning of this day do indeed belong together. The event witnessed to in our lesson and the other event here in Dallas on that dark Friday just a year ago—these two events illuminate one another and our common situation as women and men before God. My whole purpose in what follows, then, is simply to point to that mutual illumination, to bear witness to that light.

I

For many of us who were here in Dallas a year ago, the question then, as ever since, was whether and in what ways the tragic event of that time would have a future. If this strikes you as a strange question, I suggest you reflect for a moment on what you mean by a historical event. You will see, I believe, that it is the very nature of such an event to be not only something in itself, but also something for the other events that succeed it. The present is always at once a realization of possibilities inherent in the past and the presentation of yet other possibilities that can only be realized in the future. Because this is so, one must say that the future of an event, the possibilities it presents for realization, actually belong to the event itself. A common way of saying this is that every event has a meaning or significance. Since to every event there belongs a future of possibilities, every event has a potential meaning that is concretely actualized with the actualization of those possibilities.

But we all know that such actualization is always the task of the future, never that of the past. What kind of a future an event is to have— even, indeed, whether it is to have any future at all—is not anything that it itself can decide. All sorts of things happen that, humanly speaking, seem to have almost no future at all. They are ignored or forgotten by those who come after them—or else are experienced as having only some trivial part of their potential meaning.

> But of others there is no memory;
> they have perished as though
> they had never existed;
> they have become as though they
> had never been born,
> they and their children after
> them.

Now, as I said, the question in the minds of many of us in Dallas has been as to the future of President Kennedy's assassination. At first, the prospects that his death would be seen as significant seemed good. No one who lived through those first two or three days in the city could fail to see that, for person after person, that event had become a moment of truth. As someone put it at the time, "Last Friday at 12:45 p.m. we all felt guilty, and we all knew why." Regardless of the hand that had held the assassin's gun, we knew that ours was in fact a city in which we had allowed intolerance and even violence to become part of our public life. The proof of this, if any were needed, was the mood of anxious apprehension in which we had awaited the President's visit. Then, when the awful "incident" actually happened, all our fears were confirmed, and we were shocked into recognizing the guilt in which each of us shared.

But this initial response was not destined to last. With the horror of murder following upon murder, it was as though we had been given to see more of ourselves than we could bear. As long as I live, I shall never forget the groan of despair that rose from our congregation that Sunday morning when our minister announced to us that Lee Harvey Oswald, too, had been shot. At any rate, within days of the original tragedy, contrition gave way to defensiveness, and there began the sorry spectacle of Dallas bent on saving the face of Dallas.

This was prompted in part, no doubt, by irresponsible arraignments of the whole city for what the city as a whole had not, in fact, done. Yet clearly the few false charges that Dallas was an accomplice in the actual crime were not the main reason for the protestations of innocence that began to be heard from some of our spokesmen. No, the matter was more complex. Some of us had begun to conclude that too candid an acknowledgment of our real guilt would be damaging to our "image" as a city and thus threaten that business and civic growth in which we've come to take such stock. At the same time, many of us—some, perhaps, having even felt pangs of guilt and remorse—were simply unwilling to bring forth fruits meet for repentance. For one reason or another, we resisted the amendment of life that a facing of the truth always requires and were anxious to return to normal as though nothing had happened.

I should not venture to say to what extent this attempt to forget the past and to deny it a future has at last come to prevail throughout the Dallas community. Sometimes I get the impression that, so far as most of us here are concerned, President Kennedy really did die in vain because the significance of his death is realized, if at all, only in ways that are trivial. Some of you may recall the moving statement of Governor Connally when he spoke publicly for the first time after the assassination from his bed at Parkland Hospital. He'd been reflecting, he told his interviewer, on why he had been spared, while the President had been taken. And the only answer he had found, he said, was that maybe the President has been asked to do something in death that he couldn't do in life—namely, so to shock and stun all of us as a nation that we would turn away from the hatred and intolerance that are the only "genesis of our self-destruction if we're ever going to be destroyed." The thought that keeps crossing my mind is whether, even in Dallas, the death of President Kennedy has had anything like this kind of an effect—or whether, as I sometimes fear, most of us have simply let it slip into a past that no longer concerns us.

On the other hand, I suspect all of us have had experiences that are more reassuring. In my own case, anyhow, there have been several such experiences, although none more memorable than one I had only a couple of weeks ago on Election Day, 1964, almost a year after the assassination.

Like many of us in the School of Theology, I had volunteered to work that day somewhere in a precinct in any way I could be helpful. As it happened, I was assigned to an area in the west of the city where I wound up driving people who wanted to vote to their polling places and then back to their homes. In one case, I was asked simply to take a woman home who had already voted and had been promised a ride back. When she got in my car and I asked where I could take her, I was surprised to learn that she no longer lived in the immediate vicinity, but had recently moved to Oak Cliff. Having failed to record her change of address in the time allowed, she had been able to vote only by coming all the way back across the city to her former precinct.

Obviously, I thought, here's someone for whom the right to vote means a great deal. To have come all that way by bus and in a drenching rain could only mean that she was far more serious than many of the rest of us. And as we talked, it became clear that this was in fact the case. Her political loyalties were strong, and she had known exactly what she had to do. But the thing that sticks in my mind is the simple, matter-of-fact witness she bore to how all this had come about. Like most other Negroes in the South, she said, she had at first had little interest in politics or even in voting. This, like everything else, was a white man's affair, and her voice wouldn't be heard anyway. But then had come the event of 22 November 1963. All at once, she confessed, she knew that her attitude was wrong. "If he could give his life for our country, then I knew the least I could do was vote!" And so, on a rainy afternoon almost a year later, this woman had kept covenant with that event and with herself and had voted.

I don't think there's any question that similar things have occurred many times over throughout the city of Dallas and elsewhere in the nation. I don't mean, of course, that what this woman saw in President Kennedy's death is the same meaning that others, too, have seen in it. I mean simply that others also have found it to be a significant event and have thus given it a future in their lives. They haven't just ignored or forgotten it—or remembered it merely as an event in the past that has no bearing on their own responsibilities in the present. Rather, they have seen it as a sign, a sign somehow intended for them, to guide them in their own decisions about how to lead their lives here and now.

When I said before that the question asked by many of us has been whether President Kennedy's death would have a future, this was the question I had in mind: To what extent would his death not only be something in itself, but also something for us—not only an event that belonged to the past, but also a sign addressed to us in the present? As I see it, this is also the question that each of us must put to her- or himself today as we pause to commemorate that event.

II

But now you're probably wondering what all this has to do with the lesson we heard read from John's Gospel. How can the event of the President's assassination in any way illumine, or be illumined by, that other event proclaimed to us in our lesson? Isn't it only too obvious that these two events are totally different—in fact, completely incommensurable? Isn't the one simply a natural happening in our ordinary secular history, whose meaning, if any, is quite ambiguous, visible to some, yet hidden to others—while the other stands before us as a divine revelation, visible to all in its utter unambiguity as a supernatural miracle?

I recognize that there are good reasons behind such questions. Christians, certainly, are without excuse for overlooking the radical difference between these two events. John Kennedy is not some kind of latter-day Christ-figure, and to suppose otherwise is, from the standpoint of Christian faith, to commit idolatry. Yet, true as this is, I'm convinced that we shall never understand the difference between these events rightly until we see the one fundamental respect in which they're exactly alike.

It is the very essence of the Christian confession to claim that God is revealed to us through certain events in our ordinary human history, and that the eyes of faith alone are able to see God's revelation. In other words, the event of Jesus of Nazareth, exactly like that of President Kennedy's assassination, is an event whose future among us is always in question. Its deeper meaning is not something it has in itself, which anyone can unambiguously read off from it. Rather, its meaning is the possibility it re-presents to us for understanding ourselves before God, a possibility that each of us must realize for her- or himself by our own ever-new decisions of faith.

But, surely, you may think, this cannot be the teaching of the passage read from the Gospel of John. Isn't its whole point to narrate a miracle, which in its very obviousness was enough to evoke a confession of faith from those who saw it?

Well, let's agree that the passage does indeed tell of a miracle. Like the other gospel writers, who, in their ways, also tell the same story, John clearly presents the feeding of the five thousand as a miraculous event

39

in Jesus' ministry. As a matter of fact, as he tells it, the element of the miraculous in the story is, if anything, heightened. Thus he comments on Jesus' initial question to Philip about how the multitude is to be fed, "This he said to test him, for he himself knew what he would do" (v. 6). We may also agree that John makes clear that the miracle was not without its effect on those who witnessed it. "When the people saw the sign that he had done, they said, 'This is indeed the prophet who is to come into the world'" (v. 14).

But we would be utterly mistaken if we supposed that John understands this response of the people to be the response proper to faith. It's true, to be sure, that the passage as read fails to make this clear. But, then, no passage can be interpreted except in its context if we're serious about rightly understanding it. And in this case, the context is absolutely crucial. In the very next verse after those we heard read, John continues: "When Jesus realized that they were about to come and take him by force to make him king, he withdrew again to the mountain by himself" (v. 15). Then, some verses later, we read: "When they found him on the other side of the sea, they said to him, 'Rabbi, when did you come here?' Jesus answered them, 'Very truly, I tell you, you are looking for me, not because you saw signs, but because you ate your fill of the loaves. Do not work for the food that perishes, but for the food that endures for eternal life'" (vv. 25–27).

Now John's point in this is pretty clear, isn't it? The response of the people to Jesus' miraculous act is not, as he understands it, the response of faith at all. They do not really see the miracle as a "sign," which poses for them the radical question of their own self-understanding, but rather respond to it on an altogether different plane. They see it merely as proof that Jesus is one who can meet their needs for "the food that perishes" and whom they therefore want to make king. But this is to say that John has no intention whatever of presenting the miracle as something unambiguous, whose meaning is plain for all to see. On the contrary, he knows, as Søren Kierkegaard came to know eighteen hundred years later, that a miracle is at best an attention-getter, a way of posing the question of faith, not a reason for answering it. What the miraculous feeding does, whether as event or as story, is simply to create a situation of decision—namely, the same situation in which we're placed by Jesus' words later in the chapter: "I am the bread of life. Whoever comes to me will never be hungry, and whoever believes in me will never be thirsty" (v. 35). Whether these words are true, whether Jesus really is "the food that endures to eternal life," is not anything that a miracle can decide. At most, it can put to us the question, which each of us must then answer for her- or himself by a free and responsible decision.

If we had time, we would discover that just this understanding of the miraculous is the consistent teaching of John's entire Gospel. Thus we would find it expressed, for instance, in the famous story of doubting Thomas that is presented in chapter 20 (vv. 24–29). Clearly, what is arresting about this story is not that Thomas is given a miraculous proof of Jesus' resurrection, but what Jesus says in response to Thomas's confession: "Have you believed because you have seen me? Blessed are those who have not seen and yet have come to believe."

But the main thing I'm concerned we understand should already be clear. For many of us today, the miracle stories in the New Testament, such as the one in this passage, pose peculiar problems. In fact, we might as well face it: we simply find it impossible to accept them as straightforward reports of actual events. Then, if we're at all sophisticated about New Testament history, we know that this isn't the way to accept them, anyhow. They're really expressions of the faith of the earliest church and serve the purpose of proclaiming its witness to Jesus Christ. But even when we're quite sure of all this, we may still wonder whether we can ever accept this witness for ourselves. Isn't the belief in miracles somehow a part of faith in Jesus Christ? And isn't our inability to believe in them why this faith must ever remain strange to us?

If the Gospel of John is right, the answer to these questions is "No!" The whole implication of our lesson, when read in context, is that belief in miracles is one thing, faith in Jesus Christ, something else. Although John seems to be free from our modern difficulties with miracles and apparently accepts them as actual events, he is completely clear that such acceptance has no bearing whatever on the decision of faith. The feeding of the five thousand is at best a sign, which is just as ambiguous and open to misunderstanding as the event to which it points. Therefore, whether we think of it as an event that actually happened or as a creation of the church's faith, the only crucial question remains unanswered. Whether Jesus is to have a future in my life, indeed, is to determine my understanding of myself before God—this I still have to decide in my own responsible freedom.

And here, it seems to me, is where the event of President Kennedy's death throws light on the event of Jesus. It presents us, so to speak, with a concrete parable of that event as an event of divine revelation.

I'm convinced that nothing so keeps us from understanding the event of Christ as our thinking of it as something utterly special, without any real analogy in the rest of our experience. We fail to see that it, too, is a happening in the very midst of our secular history, whose significance is far from obvious and whose future among human beings always waits on their personal decisions. It's true, as we have seen, that we never encounter the event of Jesus alone, apart from the witness of the church in which its significance for us is already made clear. But, then, what's that witness itself but simply another event in our ordinary history—a word spoken by human beings just such as ourselves, whose right to speak to us in God's name is hardly self-evident? Indeed, even the church's witness can never be more than a sign, which is no less ambiguous than the event to which it bears witness. And here, too, the parallel with that other event is illumining. For it was just such ambiguity that also characterized the simple testimony of that Black woman to the significance of President Kennedy's death for her life.

But if these events are in one respect exactly alike, in another respect, they're radically different. To begin with, the event of Jesus Christ is attested by Christian faith and witness as having a kind of significance that the other event neither has nor should be supposed to have. The question Jesus Christ poses for us is not the question of our responsibility for some particular sphere of life—say, for the social and political order that is so important to our welfare in this world. No, the question he raises is the infinitely, qualitatively different, more momentous question of our total understanding of ourselves as persons. It is the existential, or religious, question of whether we're to seek the final meaning of our life in what we ourselves are and have and do, or are to receive that meaning utterly and completely as a gift. In other words, the significance of Jesus Christ is to present us with the possibility of obedient faith in God's love. In fact, he himself actually is that love, happening in our midst as an event and demanding a decision from each one of us.

Corresponding, then, to this difference between the events themselves, there is also a difference in our possible responses to them. We give the event of Jesus Christ a future in our lives, not by performing some particular act or course of action—say, by overcoming our apathy and indifference and accepting our responsibility as citizens to vote. No, Jesus Christ comes to dwell in us, and we in him, only when we so respond to his total gift and demand that not only our particular acts and our habits, but also our very persons, are totally transformed. "If you love me, you will keep my commandments"; and "this is my commandment, that you love one another as I have loved you" (John 14:15; 15:12). Because what encounters us through Jesus Christ is the very love of God itself, we realize the significance of that event only when we ourselves become free to love in return.

And yet, just when we see the event of Jesus Christ in all its radical difference, it casts a strange new light on all the other events of our lives—including the event that, in another sense, illumines it. As someone has said, "The first task of love is to listen." We can love others only if we're willing to attend to them as they are, to take their needs into account, and to be guided in our decisions by the concrete possibilities and limitations of their situations. The reason for this lies in the very nature of love itself. Although love is never identical with any one particular act, it can never find expression except in quite specific words and deeds. If we're to love at all, it must always be through particular acts of witness and service, whereby we respond to our neighbors' actual needs both of body and of soul. But this means that everything that happens suddenly takes on a new significance. From the standpoint of faith in Jesus Christ, no event can be merely indifferent, for it is laden with meaning. It, too, is a word of God to us, which would point us the more clearly and certainly to the claim of God's love on our lives.

It's not for me to try to determine what God would say to you in the death of President Kennedy. But this much I have the authority to tell you: that, in the light of Jesus Christ, God wills to speak and to be heard also through that event. It, too, like all the other events of our experience, will be a sign for you—indeed, for all of us. Amen.

6 October 1971

Luke 14:7–11

When he noticed how the guests chose the places of honor, he told them a parable. "When you are invited by someone to a wedding banquet, do not sit down at the place of honor, in case someone more distinguished than you has been invited by your host; and the host who invited both of you may come and say to you, 'Give this person your place,' and then in disgrace you would start to take the lowest place. But when you are invited, go and sit down at the lowest place, so that when your host comes, he may say to you, 'Friend, move up higher'; then you will be honored in the presence of all who sit at the table with you. For all who exalt themselves will be humbled, and those who humble themselves will be exalted."

In this second half of our New Testament lesson, we're presented with one of the most transparent parables in the synoptic tradition. At any rate, the Evangelist represents it as a parable; and the point it makes, considering the verse with which it ends, is as obvious as the point of the other Parable of the Pharisee and the Tax Collector, which he concludes, as you may remember, with the very same verse (cf. 18:9–14).

The background of the parable is human society as we also know it today, with its more or less clearly defined structures of status and privilege. Given such structures, Jesus warns, anyone who is prudent and interested in social mobility and advancement will do well to remember one's station. Instead of laying claim to a higher status than one deserves, and so running the risk of being outclassed and publicly embarrassed by someone more eminent, one should, if anything, understate one's claims,

44

and so possibly have the satisfaction of eventually being advanced. Far better to claim little and hope for promotion than to be overly ambitious and expose oneself to the humiliation of being demoted.

We've all had sufficient experience to recognize the prudence of this warning. For us today, even as for persons in Jesus' day, our life in society must constantly take into account the various status structures, apart from which such life is impossible. Nor is this a mere historical contingency that might have been otherwise. Say as we will that "One person is as good as another," the all too obvious truth is that we're far from being equal with respect either to our native talents or to our eventual contributions to society and culture. Spanning our inequality, of course, is our common endowment with the gift of thought and speech, and thus with the capacity to lead our lives in a wide variety of ways in terms of meaningful concepts and symbols; and this establishes sufficient mutuality between all of us to make any hierarchical ranking according to our individual worth at best relative and usually open to question. Even so, there are enough differences between each of us and every other that the shape of society, with its differences of function and status, is far from being merely accidental.

This is nowhere more evident than right here in the University and in the Divinity School. Here, too, differences in rank and distinction among both faculty and students are an ever-present fact of life. There are full professors and research associates, mature scholars whose competence is already proven and others who are only just beginning to fulfill the promise of their scholarly careers. And, among students, there are those who are recognized and honored by all for their academic achievement, as well as those who have to struggle throughout the whole term of their study simply to meet the minimal requirements for getting their degrees.

In this context, we can all understand the background of Jesus' parable—even, possibly, only too well! Not so long ago, I was speaking with a recent college graduate who has since gone on for graduate study at a well-known eastern university. He confessed his almost chronic anxiety at having to establish his standing in the academic community all over again. In college he was a Phi Beta Kappa, recognized by faculty and students alike as one of the best students there. In graduate school, on the other hand, he's learned that he's simply one more student, along with any number of others of equal or even superior distinction; and it's been far from self-evident that he will ever be able to attain a standing in that community comparable to the one he previously enjoyed. He certainly could understand, as I take it all of us can, what Jesus takes for granted about our life in society when he says, "all who exalt themselves will be humbled, and those who humble themselves will be exalted."

To be sure, we all know that this rule has many exceptions in society as we experience it. There are those, both in this community and in others, who enjoy a higher status than they have any right to claim. One of the recurrent problems of our whole social life is that there are always those whose function in the community may have once earned a high position of status and privilege, but who continue to occupy that position even after they no longer perform the function—at any rate, not very well. And we hardly need to be told that the ambitious person who claims a higher status than she or he deserves as often as not succeeds in making good her or his claim. Even if the well-known "Peter principle" had never been formulated, it would have been a fair guess that all too many positions are filled by those who have risen to the level of their incompetence. It is just not so that "all who exalt themselves will be humbled," any more than it's true, in the same obvious sense, that "all who take the sword will perish by the sword" (Matt 26:52). Time and again, it's precisely one who exalts oneself who is exalted. As a matter of fact, it often seems that such a one is the only one who's exalted! Nor would any of us have the least difficulty in thinking of exceptions to the second half of Jesus' statement as well. So far from always eventually being advanced, the humble person as often as not simply gets lost in the rush. In the world as we all know it, the humble and meek are not always exalted, any more than the proud and mighty are always scattered in the imaginations of their hearts.

And yet, if we remember that what is presented in our text is a parable, all such exceptions are really irrelevant. We may have every confidence that the Evangelist, as much as Jesus himself, was as well aware as we are that in human society the exalted are not always humbled, any more than the humbled are always exalted. But what the parable simply takes for granted is a specific relation in which the rule in question does in fact hold good. And the reason for this is obvious: what the parable represents, although precisely as a parable, is the essential character of our status as human beings in relation to God; and here, in this one unique relationship, the rule admits of no exceptions that "all who exalt themselves will be humbled, and those who humble themselves will be exalted."

Anyone who attempts to secure one's life by what one oneself is or has or does is inevitably humbled—humbled by being given over precisely thereby to the perishing and death that are the inevitable fate of every creaturely thing and by also failing to realize in the present one's possibility before God of living a genuine human existence in freedom and love. This inevitability is not in the least the precarious inevitability, always subject to exceptions, that can alone be claimed for our life in society. Nor is it merely some kind of a transcendental analogue to such precarious inevitability, whose principal difference is that God, being omniscient and all-powerful, is able to guarantee, as society never can, that the wholly external connection between act and consequence is nevertheless secured. No, whatever the value of any such analogy, as providing, possibly, a picture of our relation to God, the truth of that relation is so radically different as to make the analogy nothing more than a picture. Indeed, it is only with this clearly in mind that we can rightly understand and apply to our own condition all such prophetic interpretations of God's dealings with Israel as we heard in our Old Testament lesson (Jer 13:15–21). Here, too, the most we have are pictures of our existence, as distinct from its actual truth as that is revealed to us through Jesus Christ.

Through him we learn that, at the deepest level of our lives, where we must somehow come to terms with the one relation in which we gain or lose ourselves as human beings, the connection between act and consequence, or between our act and God's, is wholly internal, and thus is, in the strictest sense, inevitable. Just as the ultimate punishment of any moral evil is the evil deed itself, so the ultimate humbling of our pride is our very act of being proud and boasting. Just in that act itself we perjure ourselves as to the truth of our existence, and so forfeit the possibility of being who we really are. On the other hand, and just as inevitably, anyone who humbles oneself before God is by that very fact already exalted into God's presence. Precisely in surrendering all of one's own self-contrived securities and boasting and looking solely to God's love for the ultimate meaning of one's life, one is already raised beyond death and perishing into the endless security of God's love, and so may live in freedom from the past and openness for the future.

So the word our text addresses to us is the same word that speaks to us in that other statement in the gospels that we've all heard so often: In Luke's formulation of it: "Those who try to make their life secure will lose it, but those who lose their life will keep it" (17:33; cf. Matt 10:39). If the prudent person of this world who desires to be exalted among her or his fellows had better make modest claims lest she or he suffer humiliation, anyone who would keep a genuine human life has no choice but to lose the life one has tried to secure oneself by surrendering it completely to God's gracious claim. The way to life leads through death, and only one who, as Luther tells us, is prepared to abandon all securities and step out into utter darkness can find and keep the genuine life in God's love that is the real goal of all of our seeking.

Lord, we pray that your grace may always be there for us and follow us, and enable us continually to be given to all good works; through Jesus Christ our Lord. Amen.

2 *Timothy* 2:1–13

You, then, my child, be strong in the grace that is in Christ Jesus;
and what you have heard from me through many witnesses entrust
to faithful people who will be able to teach others as well. Share in
suffering like a good soldier of Christ Jesus. No one serving in the
army gets entangled in everyday affairs; the soldier's aim is to please
the enlisting officer. And in the case of an athlete, no one is crowned
without competing according to the rules. It is the farmer who does
the work who ought to have the first share of the crops. Think over
what I say, for the Lord will give you understanding in all things.

Remember Jesus Christ, raised from the dead, a descendant of
David—that is my gospel, for which I suffer hardship, even to the
point of being chained like a criminal. But the word of God is not
chained. Therefore I endure everything for the sake of the elect, so
that they may also obtain the salvation that is in Christ Jesus, with
eternal glory. The saying is sure:

> *If we have died with him, we will also live with him;*
> *if we endure, we will also reign with him;*
> *if we deny him, he will also deny us;*
> *if we are faithless, he remains faithful—*
> *for he cannot deny himself.*

We could hardly find a more appropriate word for this occasion than
the one addressed to us in the lesson just read as the Epistle for the day.
Gathered as we are around the table of the Lord, in obedience to his com-
mand, "Do this in remembrance of me" (1 Cor 11:24), we hear the words

of our lesson, "Remember Jesus Christ, raised from the dead, a descendant of David—that is my gospel, for which I suffer hardship, even to the point of being chained like a criminal." And when we reflect further on the context in which these words are spoken, we realize at once that the word they express is indeed intended also for us. For, not unlike Timothy himself, we, too, are, in our own way, children of the Apostle who, having heard his gospel through many witnesses, have now been called out to the special ministry of teaching and preaching that gospel.

To be sure, not all of us here have been recognized in this calling by the laying on of hands, and some of us may still remain far from certain even whether it is this special ministry to which God is calling them. And yet, for all of its importance for the well-being of the church, ordination is but the sign of an office that one has only by performing it and by preparing oneself for its performance. Nor is there any other way to become certain of one's calling to that office than to measure oneself against the demands placed on every leader in the church by diligently preparing to meet them. Regardless of our office, then, and whatever the extent of our preparation for church leadership, all of us in this community—that being the very thing that makes us the school of theology we are—are among those to whom the word of our lesson is specifically addressed.

But just what is this word? Well, clearly, it is a word we can hear only as a demand—and, in one aspect, as a demand for what each of us must undertake to do by her or his own words and deeds as a free and responsible person. It is the demand, quite simply, that we be strong, that we be faithful and endure, in the special ministry of preaching and teaching the gospel that we share in this community—including the calling of some of us here to see to it that the gospel we have all received is entrusted to faithful teachers "who will be able to teach others as well." Mainly by precept but also by his own example, the Apostle summons us, too, to faithfulness in our special calling, even to the point of accepting with him our own share of suffering for the gospel and for the sake of those whom God elects by means of it. Like the soldier in service whose sole aim is to justify the trust of those who enlisted him, we are to avoid involving ourselves in any undertaking irrelevant to our mission. Or, again, we are challenged to reflect that only the hard-working farmer has a claim on a first share of the harvest, and that no athlete can expect to win and keep the victor's crown who breaks the rules of the game—by which is meant, presumably, not only the rules of the contest itself, but also the training rules, whose observance alone prepares one for the competition.

But, as both of these examples are intended to warn us, the promise attached to this first aspect of our lesson's demand is a conditional promise only. Since what is demanded of us is something that we may also always fail to do, the promise made to us also implies a threat. And this is made explicit, then, in the words of the sure saying with which our lesson concludes: only if we endure to the end in faithfulness to our calling shall we also reign with Christ, for "if we deny him, he will also deny us."

And yet, obviously, this one aspect of the demand is not its only or even most important aspect. For we are told with the first sentence of our lesson that, if we are to be strong, we are to be so not in our own power, but "in the grace that is in Christ Jesus." And no sooner are we summoned to accept our own share of suffering as good soldiers of Christ than we hear those words that are the very center of the lesson: "Remember Jesus Christ, raised from the dead, a descendant of David—that is my gospel." Of course, these words, also, place a demand on us. But it is not a demand for what only we can do by our own words and deeds, but the demand, rather, that, in all our speaking and doing, we never forget what has already been done for us by another. And in this other aspect, the promise that attaches to the demand is far more than a merely conditional promise. For, as sure as the saying is, that only if we have died with Christ shall we also live with him, the gift of the promise of life, and the deed in our history in which that gift has been given, once and for all, are in no way conditional on what we do, and much less on what we fail to do. Just as the word of God itself remains unchained even when its servant is in chains, so God through Jesus Christ ever remains faithful even if we ourselves are faithless to the demands of our calling.

Therefore, even if God does and must deny us in all our denials of God, the last words of our lesson, and so, we may claim, the surest saying of all, is that God "cannot deny Godself"—not, note well, "*will* not deny Godself," but "*can* not deny Godself," cannot deny God's own promise to be our God, which God has given to us and to the world decisively through Jesus Christ.

Not to us, O Lord, but to your name be all glory given because of your steadfast love and your faithfulness. Amen.

Luke 10:25–37

Just then a lawyer stood up to test Jesus. "Teacher," he said, "what must I do to inherit eternal life?" He said to him, "What is written in the law? What do you read there?" He answered, "You shall love the Lord your God with all your heart, and with all your soul, and with all your strength, and with all your mind; and your neighbor as yourself." And he said to him, "You have given the right answer; do this, and you will live."

But wanting to justify himself, he asked Jesus, "And who is my neighbor?" Jesus replied, "A man was going down from Jerusalem to Jericho, and fell into the hands of robbers, who stripped him, beat him, and went away, leaving him half dead. Now by chance a priest was going down that road; and when he saw him, he passed by on the other side. So likewise a Levite, when he came to the place and saw him, passed by on the other side. But a Samaritan while traveling came near him; and when he saw him, he was moved with pity. He went to him and bandaged his wounds, having poured oil and wine on them. Then he put him on his own animal, brought him to an inn, and took care of him. The next day he took out two denarii, gave them to the innkeeper, and said, 'Take care of him; and when I come back, I will repay you whatever more you spend.' Which of these three, do you think, proved a neighbor to the man who fell into the hands of the robbers?" He said, "The one who showed him mercy." Jesus said to him, "Go and do likewise."

I

Of all the traditions in the gospels, probably none is more familiar to us than those we've heard as the New Testament lesson for today. Along with the Parable of the Prodigal Son, the Parable of the Good Samaritan has always held a unique place in the church's memory of the person and event that are the principle as well as the origin of its existence as the church. And who among us this morning does not immediately associate Jesus with just that summary, or simplification, of the law in the great commandment that we shall love the Lord our God with all our heart and soul and strength and mind and our neighbor as ourselves?

But familiar as our lesson is to us in both of its parts, it's by no means obvious that we've already learned what it has to teach us—or, even if we have, that we do not need to hear its word again. In fact, its very familiarity to us may only mean that, like Christians generally, we've so assimilated and domesticated it that we're as much in need of hearing its word anew as we have failed to remember, or, perhaps, even to learn, its intended meaning.

Of course, the question is just how we're able to do this. My suggestion is that we simply follow the lead of the Evangelist Luke himself and let our own situation and question today provide the context in which we listen to our lesson. As we'll see in more detail when we take a closer look at it, Luke doesn't simply transmit the tradition he's received, but introduces a number of changes in it that evidently reflect his own situation and that of his church, as well as his own judgment as to the meaning of the gospel in and for that situation. He's not unique in this, of course, since the same thing could be said of the other evangelists. As hard as it may be for us to realize it, the tradition lying behind our gospels and eventually redacted in them was from its very beginning a tradition of preaching—thus in no way a matter of mere historical reporting, but a matter of hearing a word of judgment and grace and then speaking that word yet again in the context of a new situation with its own peculiar question. But be this as it may, not the least important change Luke makes in the tradition he has received is to disengage it to a considerable extent from its originally Jewish context. Whereas in the parallel passages in Matthew and Mark the question provoking Jesus' statement of the great commandment is the typically Jewish question about the first, or the chief, commandment, or, as Matthew has it, about "the greatest and first commandment" (Matt 22:30), in Luke's version, the lawyer makes no mention of either commandment or law but simply asks, "Teacher, what must I do to inherit eternal life?" A check of Luke's other uses of this phrase, "inheriting eternal life," makes clear that it's but another expression for "entering the kingdom of God," or "being saved" (Luke 18:24–25, 29). It's clear, then, that Luke understands the lawyer's question as one that might just as well be put by a Christian as by a Jew. This is already an indication that he intends his reader to receive the story not only as having to do with the situation and question of a Jew in the past, but also, and primarily, as illumining the reader's own situation and question in the present. And this is fully confirmed, then, by the point he obviously wants to make in retelling the story. We not only have every right, therefore, to receive Luke's own version of the story just as he received what came to him, but it's only so that we can receive the story as he intends us to receive it: as God's own word addressed to us in our situation and with our own distinctive question.

But if this is how we're to hear our lesson, our first task, clearly, is to take a closer look at the lesson itself; and in this connection there are a number of observations we need to make.

II

The first has to do with the opening of the lesson. It is significant that down through the centuries in which it has been read in the church, it has traditionally begun, not with v. 25, with the lawyer's test question to Jesus, but two verses earlier, where Jesus is represented as saying to the disciples, "Blessed are the eyes that see what you see! For I tell you that many prophets and kings desired to see what you see, but did not see it, and to hear what you hear, but did not hear it." It's against the background of this claim by Jesus for the decisive significance of his own ministry that Luke proceeds with the words, "Just then a lawyer stood up to test Jesus." So, as Luke presents it, the story of Jesus' encounter with the lawyer seems to be by way of making clear just wherein Jesus' decisive significance is to be seen. The test question that the lawyer puts to him is, in effect, a challenge to the claim that Jesus has just made for his own ministry as itself a blessing long desired by prophets and kings. But if this is correct, all that follows on the lawyer's initial question ought to make sense if read as Jesus' response to this challenge. In other words, whatever else we're to learn from our lesson, it ought to teach us something about who Jesus is and what we're therefore to understand by his extraordinary claim.

The second observation is that Luke evidently views all the rest of the lesson as an integral unity having a single unified meaning. The pertinence of this observation is that the rest of the lesson is, in fact, a literary composition of materials that is unique to Luke's Gospel. Although its first part has parallels in the treatments of the great commandment by both Matthew and Mark, the Parable of the Good Samaritan, which makes up its second part, occurs only in the Gospel of Luke. But, different as they doubtless were in the form in which Luke received them, he has now brought the two units of tradition together into a tight literary unity.

This is already clear from the fact that he represents them as but two stages in a single interchange that is initiated by the lawyer's original question. Thus at each stage, the formal pattern of the interchange is the same: the lawyer puts a question only to be met with Jesus' counterquestion; and the lawyer's reply in turn meets with the same kind of a response from Jesus: "Do this, and you will live" (v. 28) and "Go and do likewise" (v. 37). In keeping with this basic pattern, then, is the most striking change that Luke introduces into his version of the great commandment. Whereas in both Matthew's and Mark's versions, it is Jesus who is represented as stating the commandment, in Luke's version, it is the lawyer himself who is made to state it. Thus Jesus' role throughout the lesson is very different from that of the great teacher who brings some new unheard of truth to his hearers. All that the lawyer ever learns from Jesus is what he himself already knows—either on the basis of what he's already learned from his religious heritage, as regards the commandment that leads to life, or on the basis of what he knows simply as a human being who himself depends on the mercy of others, as regards the identity of his neighbor. What role is assigned to Jesus, then? Well, throughout the lesson, in one part as well as in the other, Jesus is the one whose counterquestions thrust his hearer back on what he already knows and who then confronts him with the summons, "Do it!"

Then there is the obvious thematic unity of the lesson, which belongs to it because both parts alike have to do with love of the neighbor. Of course, Luke follows the tradition he's received by also speaking of love of God. To Jesus' counterquestions, "What is written in the law? What do you read there?" the lawyer answers, "You shall love the Lord your God with all your heart, and with all your soul, and with all your strength, and with all your mind; and your neighbor as yourself" (vv. 26–27). But here, also, there's a singular difference in Luke's version of the tradition. Unlike Matthew's and Mark's, there is no enumeration of a first commandment and a second commandment, nor is there any stress on the essential equality of the two commandments such as Matthew introduces by saying, "And a second is like it: you shall love your neighbor as yourself" (Matt 22:39). Instead, there's just one occurrence of the verb, "You shall love," which has neighbor as well as God as its object. In this way, too, Luke creates a unified meaning for the entire passage. By speaking, in effect, of but one commandment, he makes clear that the meaning of the law is one and the same with the love of the neighbor concretely done by the Samaritan in the parable.

This leads to some final observations on the parable itself. No doubt the most striking thing about it is that it is a Samaritan who is the subject of neighbor love, while the man who is its object is evidently understood to be a Jew. This is particularly striking, since the basic point of the parable, that neighbor love breaks through all barriers of race and religion, could still be made if the roles were reversed. After all, it would require no less freedom from conventional restrictions on the scope of neighbor love for a Jew to love a Samaritan than vice versa. But, if we recall that the parable is an integral part of the lesson as a whole, the way it's in fact told is hardly accidental. Nor is the reason for it simply that, as many commentators have noted, Jesus tells the story precisely in order to force the lawyer back on his own experience, and so wants him to identify immediately and completely with the man who fell among robbers—an identification that he might not be as likely to make were the man a Samaritan instead of a Jew. No, important as that doubtless is to the psychological dynamics of the story, the deeper reason for the Samaritan's being the one who loves is that it's the actual doing of love, not the mere knowledge that it's to be done, that is the one central point in the entire lesson.

From the standpoint of a Jew, a Samaritan was not only racially impure but also religiously heterodox. Although Samaritans acknowledged the authority of the first five books of the law, they acknowledged nothing else in the Hebrew Scriptures and, beyond that, were held to be wildly irregular in cultic practice and ritual observance. But, clearly, the whole point of the lesson—which is also underscored by the fact that it's precisely a priest and a Levite who pass by on the other side—is that neither correct knowledge of the law nor cultic and ritual propriety is of any avail, but only the love of the neighbor that does what the law requires by responding to the neighbor's actual needs. Just as Jesus' only role throughout the lesson is to summon his hearers to the actual doing of the love that they already know to be required of them, so the fact that the subject of love is a despised Samaritan removes all doubt as to the only role of Jesus' hearers if they're to respond to his summons.

And this is further borne out by another feature of the parable that's often missed. Most commentators have drawn attention to the difference between the meaning of the word "neighbor" in the lawyer's question, "And who is my neighbor?" and the meaning it has in Jesus' counterquestion, on the basis of his parable, "Which of these three, do you think, proved a neighbor to the man who fell into the hands of the robbers?" Whereas the neighbor about whom the lawyer asks is the *object* of neighbor love, the one to whom love is to be done, the neighbor about whom Jesus asks is, rather, the *subject* of such love, the one who is to do the love. But, important as this difference is to the whole point of the lesson, even more important is the other shift of meaning that takes place between the two questions. Whereas "neighbor" as the lawyer understands the word is a matter of status or position—of who one *is*—"neighbor" as Jesus understands it is entirely a matter of role or function—of what one *does*. Thus, significantly, his question asks not, which of these three *was* a neighbor to the man who fell among robbers, but, rather, which of these three *proved* a neighbor to him—namely, by the concrete deed of love in face of his actual needs. In this way, also, the single point of the entire lesson is driven home: what counts, finally, is not what one knows but what one does, not what one already is, but what one ever again proves to be in one's encounter with one's fellow human beings in their need for one's help.

III

We should be ready now to try to listen to our lesson again, asking our own question as it arises in our situation today. As different as we may be from the lawyer in a number of respects, there are other, more fundamental respects in which we readily identify with him. We, too, stand in a religious heritage in which the basic human question, "What shall I do to attain authentic life?" has already been raised and given an answer. Moreover, we belong to just that segment of our society that is more or less knowledgeable of this religious heritage. Not many of us, of course, would claim to be professional theologians or students of religion. But the very fact that we're here in this place, gathered for this occasion, means that we not only stand in a religious tradition but are also, to some extent, thoughtful about it. Indeed, it's quite likely that we've thought enough about it that we can no longer simply accept religious claims without question. We've acquired something of an intellectual conscience even in matters of religion, and so find ourselves disposed to challenge all such claims in the interest of religious truth.

And this is our situation when we're confronted with the astonishing claim of Jesus, or of the church that claims to speak in his name, for the decisive significance of his ministry. "Blessed are the eyes that see what you see! For I tell you that many prophets and kings desired to see what you see, but did not see it, and to hear what you hear, but did not hear it." Perhaps we've already credited this claim and, in one way or another, think of ourselves as Christians. But even then the insistent demands of our intellectual conscience may drive us to seek an understanding of the claim that will allow us to vindicate its truth. So, even if we've already accepted it, or are disposed to accept it, we find ourselves in effect challenging it by putting Jesus to the test. "If you're who you claim to be," we ask, "what answer do you give to the age-old religious question? What do you say I must do to attain an authentic human life?"

Yet, far from answering our question, Jesus forces us to answer it ourselves. "You stand in a religious heritage and are knowledgeable about it," he says. "What does it say you must do? And what do you make of that?" Obviously, the only answer we can honestly give is essentially the same as the lawyer's. For, although our religious heritage may be more universal than his, what it says to us, and what we're forced to make of it, is hardly different. Everywhere, in all the so-called higher religions, we're met with the same teaching that, if we would live, we must love. But if Jesus teaches us nothing we haven't learned already, or, at least, could have learned, what can be so decisive about his ministry? Well, what could be decisive about it but that word of demand and promise that is his only response to our answer? "Do this, and you will live." Although he in no way tells us what to do beyond what we already know to be required of us, he confronts us anew with the same requirement and then confirms the promise that it is the commandment to love that leads to life.

And yet, this, too, is almost certain to raise a question for us—a question not all that different, after all, from the lawyer's. For it's one of the paradoxes of every religious heritage that it can give an answer to our human question about authentic life only by also tending to obscure it. Just because it is in *this* religious heritage that the answer is given, it itself acquires a peculiar importance that sets it apart from everything else. It itself comes to share in the sacred, while everything else remains secular or profane. Then all the beliefs, rites, and forms of organization that are essential to it themselves take on special significance, with the result that new limits come to be set to the scope of neighbor love. "Who, then, is my neighbor?" we ask. "Is it every other human being who is somehow moved, much as I am, by the question of authentic life? Or is it only the fellow heir of my own religious heritage who, like me, accepts its answer to this question?"

That this is a real question for us as well as for those who first encountered Jesus is clear enough. Already in the New Testament, love of the neighbor comes to be understood primarily, if not exclusively, as love of the "brother" (or the "sister"), which is to say, the fellow Christian. And so it's been down through the Christian centuries right up to the present. Although every human person is in a sense acknowledged to be the neighbor, there's always that qualification, "in a sense." The special object of Christian love is the fellow-member of the household of faith, even if we're also commanded to do good to all human beings as we have opportunity (cf. Gal 6:10). Nor can we avoid the question simply by appealing beyond Christianity to the more universal heritage of the higher religions generally. For, as we today have particular reason to realize, there is still the barrier between those who are religious in one way or another and those who profess to be out and out secularists, rejecting religion altogether. Is the secularist also my neighbor?

There's no possibility of answering our second question, then, by simply falling back on our religious heritage. And so, not surprisingly it is not to it that Jesus refers us. Instead, he tells a parable, thereby forcing us to look beyond all our religious knowledge to the deeper level of our own experience, where the answer to the question, "Who is my neighbor?" never ceases to press in upon us. Simply in knowing our own need as human beings, that we ourselves are always at the mercy of others, we know that our neighbor is anyone near enough for us to be of help, and that we ourselves only prove to be neighbors as and when we offer it.

And this is not all that we learn when Jesus' parable forces us to look down into the depths of our own experience. For, in learning who our neighbor is, and what it means for us ourselves to prove neighbors, we also learn who God is. A teacher of mine liked to say, "You can always tell who someone's real God is by what makes her or his face red!" In the same vein, I like to say that the real God whom someone worships is always revealed by those whom she or he acknowledges as neighbors—acknowledges as neighbors not merely in theory or by defining their status or position, but in the concrete acts of human helpfulness whereby one can alone prove a neighbor to them. We learn, in other words, that there is more to Luke's reduction of the two commandments to one than any mere conventions of literary unity. What he expresses in the lesson is the deep theological truth that we already know in our own hearts: that we can love neither God nor our neighbor except insofar as we love both, and that the only proof of our love for the God who alone can claim all our heart and soul and all our strength and mind is to meet any human need that confronts us for no other reason than that it is there to be met and that we are there and able to meet it.

Yet if we always already know even this—both who our neighbor is and who God is—what can warrant Jesus' claim for the decisive significance of his ministry? What, then, is the blessing of his presence among us that prophets and kings looked forward to but did not see or hear? Well, once again, the only thing that it could be is that his is not only the counterquestion that forces us to the full knowledge of ourselves but also the decisive word that responds to our only honest answer by summoning us to do what we know. "Go and do likewise!" Only this time, Jesus' word to us is more than a demand and a promise. Although it, too, confronts us anew with the one commandment that has always claimed us and promised us life, it also bids us as the single individual each of us is to fulfill that commandment in the trust that we're now free to do so. Jesus' last word to each of us, in short, is also a word of grace: an invitation, in spite of all our past failures to love, to enter the world of the good Samaritan, the world in which all of us both are and can be neighbors to one another because God Godself has always already proved neighbor to us all—embracing each of us in love, and so freeing us to love in return.

But this is to say, simply, that Jesus's ministry is the very deed of God's own love as something expressly done to us in our history. In this sense, he himself proves to be our good Samaritan. For the blessing of his presence among us even now is that the love that we know to be our only authentic life is no longer merely known but done: done both as God's deed of love for us and, so far as we trust God's word of grace, as our own deed of love for one another. "Go, then, and do likewise!" Amen.

Ephesians 1:15–23

I have heard of your faith in the Lord Jesus and your love toward all the saints, and for this reason I do not cease to give thanks for you as I remember you in my prayers. I pray that the God of our Lord Jesus Christ, the Father of glory, may give you a spirit of wisdom and revelation as you come to know him, so that, with the eyes of your heart enlightened, you may know what is the hope to which he has called you, what are the riches of his glorious inheritance among the saints, and what is the immeasurable greatness of his power for us who believe, according to the working of his great power. God put this power to work in Christ when he raised him from the dead and seated him at his right hand in the heavenly places, far above all rule and authority and power and dominion, and above every name that is named, not only in this age but also in the age to come. And he has put all things under his feet and has made him the head over all things for the church, which is his body, the fullness of him who fills all in all.

I

You will probably have already been reminded by our lessons that today is what has traditionally been called the Sunday after Ascension and, in the new United Methodist version of the Christian year, is called, simply, Ascension Sunday. But if you listened carefully to the lessons, to what they seem to be all about, you will probably also have been reminded of the difficulties that many of us today are likely to have with them. I don't mean, of course, that each of us has such difficulties so far as her or his own personal belief is concerned—although I suspect that many of us in this congregation do have them. But I think we are all aware that the traditional Christian belief in Christ's ascension into heaven has become a problem today for many persons to whom we are called to bear our witness of faith. Where they do not simply ignore or silently reject it, they accept it as a mere belief, whose bearing on our actual life, if any, is far from clear even in the case of those who are most insistent on their affirming it.

I cannot hope to clear up such difficulties here, even if I supposed (as I do not) that a sermon is the proper place in which to try to do so. But I do have some confidence that, if we listen again to what is said in our Epistle for today, and follow up the questions it forces us to raise, we, too, may be able to hear the word of God on this Ascension Sunday.

II

You'll recall that the larger context of our lesson is what, in form, at least, is a letter of the Apostle Paul to a gentile church, which has traditionally been identified as the church at Ephesus. Most scholars today not only doubt that Paul was the author of the letter but also regard it as having been originally addressed, not to some particular congregation, but to the church at large—its form as a letter being but a literary fiction and its address to Ephesus being almost certainly due to the title assigned to the writing only later and having no warrant in the best manuscript evidence still available to us. But, be all this as it may, what is said in the writing, and so also in our lesson, was evidently intended by its author to be the authoritative word of the Apostle to some, if not all, gentile Christians— Christians who, though they were not members of God's old covenant with Israel, and thus once were far off, have now been brought near, being incorporated into the church by hearing and believing "the word of truth, the gospel of [their] salvation" (1:13).

In this context, then, what we find in our lesson is this: having heard of the faith in the Lord Jesus of those to whom he is writing, the Apostle tells them of the place they have in his prayers—prayers not only of thanksgiving but also of intercession. "I do not cease to give thanks for you," he says, asking that "the God of our Lord Jesus Christ, the Father of glory, may give you a spirit of wisdom and revelation as you come to know him." By thus making his intercession for them, the Apostle is, in effect, confronting his readers with a challenge—just as any sincere prayer of intercession involves not only a commitment to action on the part of the one praying it, but calls for others to act as well, in some cases, the very ones for whom one is praying.

But to what action are the Apostle's readers in effect challenged? Judging from what he's already said, one can only answer that they're challenged to achieve a real knowledge of God: to accept God's gift of "a spirit of wisdom and revelation" as they come to know God. Yet isn't this an odd challenge, seeing that the readers are already Christians, of whose faith the Apostle himself has heard, and who, therefore, must already know God? I don't find it odd at all, given the assumptions of the lesson. To be sure, the readers are already Christians, of whose faith the Apostle has heard. But what kind of a faith is it about which he could possibly hear? Is it that deep, innermost trust and loyalty of the heart of whose presence, or absence, God alone can be the judge? Or is it simply whatever of such deep faith could have become publicly known through their outward words and deeds? It's evidently only the second, and yet what the Apostle says he prays for, and what he thereby challenges his readers to achieve, is something other and more than this. He prays, he says, that the eyes of their hearts may be enlightened—in other words, that their knowledge of God may be more than something merely in their heads or their outward behavior by becoming, as we would say today, *existential*: not only the knowledge that there is a God in general, but the innermost trust in and loyalty to that God as *my* God.

That this is, in fact, the meaning of the lesson is confirmed by what it is that the eyes of the readers' hearts are to know once they're enlightened—namely, the hope to which God has called them, the riches of his glorious inheritance among the saints, and the immeasurable greatness of his power for us who believe. Whatever else may be meant by the knowledge of God—such knowledge, say, as philosophy may seek and find—the knowledge of God that is the core of all theistic religion and faith is always this kind of existential knowledge, the knowledge of God as the primal source and the final end of our own individual existence, and hence the object of our hope, our final inheritance, and the last power by which our lives here and now are already determined. As Luther put it unforgettably in his exegesis of the First Commandment, "A god is that to which we can look for all good and in which we find refuge in every time of need. To have a god is nothing else than to trust and believe him with our whole heart . . . For these two belong together: faith and God. That to which your heart clings and entrusts itself is, I say, really your God." What the Apostle challenges his readers to achieve, then, is this kind of faith in God, this knowledge of God in their hearts as the ultimate meaning of their own existence.

Yet this by itself is a purely formal challenge, which raises the question of just who this God is whom the readers are to know in this existential way. So, not surprisingly, the Apostle immediately addresses himself to this question: What is the power, you ask, that is at work in your own faith as the ultimate meaning of your existence? Well, it's the very power that raised Christ from the dead and seated him in the heavenly places, far above all other powers, whatever they may be called, whether in this world or in the world to come. The God that I pray you shall come to know as your God, the Apostle tells them, is the God who has put all things under the feet of Christ and given him to be the supreme head of the church.

Of course, it's just here that the language of our lesson gives rise to those difficulties for many today that we began by frankly acknowledging. And this becomes all the more obvious if we understand that language in the literal sense in which it is actually used in our lesson. For, contrary to what we today may suppose, the reference here to "rule and authority and power and dominion" is not at all to such merely secular or worldly things as we usually intend by the same words. The literal meaning of the reference is fully brought out only when we take each of these words, "rule" and "authority," and "power" and "dominion," to refer to a certain kind of supernatural being, and thus translate, as Moffatt does in his version, "angelic Rulers, Authorities, Powers, and Lords," all in caps. In other words, there isn't the least question that the picture that our lesson calls to mind is a thoroughly mythological picture of the world as peopled with all sorts of divine or quasi-divine and demonic powers that play a fateful role in human destiny. And, of course, the distinction it assumes between this present age and the age to come, along with the whole image of Christ's being raised from the dead and exalted to God's right hand above all these cosmic powers, belongs to this same mythological world-picture.

But is there any question in your minds, really, about what the Apostle wishes to say in speaking in such mythological language? Isn't his point quite simply to say that, whatever powers there may be either in this world or in the next, the only final and all-determining power, to which all of them are subject, is the power that makes itself known to us through Jesus Christ and is even now present in his body the church? In short, isn't the witness that is borne here to Christ's ascension by way of making clear who God is, and thus who we as Christians are challenged to know not only with the eyes of our minds, but also with the eyes of our hearts?

This, in any case, is what I take to be the meaning of the witness, and I think much the same may be said of all the other New Testament assertions of Christ's ascension, including the one we heard in our Gospel lesson this morning (Luke 24:44–53). To assert that Christ is ascended into heaven is, most fundamentally, to make a certain assertion about who God is. It is to assert, in the words of our lesson itself, that "the Father of glory" is none other than "the God of our Lord Jesus Christ," which is to say, that the really ultimate power with which not only we but all women and men have to do is the power that makes itself known to us, and will, through us, be known to them, too, through the Jesus whom we as Christians confess to be the Christ: the anointed One of God

III

Yet, if this is right, the crucial question that our lesson raises for us is a question that it by itself does not answer—namely, Who, then, is Jesus Christ? Who is this one through whom God Godself is decisively re-presented, through whom the ultimate meaning of our own existence is made known? (I remark, parenthetically, that this is, in fact, the crucial question raised by all talk of Jesus' ascension. For, strange as we may find it today, there's nothing at all singular, much less distinctively Christian, in the bare idea of someone's ascending into heaven. In the ancient world in which the Christian witness of faith was first formulated, this was an utterly familiar idea—ascensions, just like resurrections and virgin births, being, as it were, perfectly natural occurrences. This is why, in that world, what was striking about the Christian assertion was not that Jesus *ascended into heaven*, but that *Jesus* ascended into heaven. *He* it was who was the subject of the assertion, the whole idea of his ascension being but one of many different predicates by which the early church tried to bear witness to their faith in his decisive significance.)

But, to go back to our question of just who Jesus is, I hope you'll understand if I risk what may seem to be a hasty or even a dogmatic answer. The Jesus who is attested to us by the earliest witness of the Christian community is the one whose entire existence, as that community remembered and expressed it, said but one thing—was, if you will, but a single word: the ultimate meaning of our existence is the boundless love of God, and the one demand that that love makes on each and every one of us is that we wholly entrust ourselves to it and, in the freedom that it makes possible, loyally serve its only cause by loving our neighbors as ourselves. To assert that *Jesus* is the ascended Lord, then, is to assert that this word that he both speaks and is is true, that the only final power over all things is God's unbegun and unending love, and that it is this love that God wills to give to every human being, demanding only that she or he accept it through obedient faith.

IV

But now, with this answer to our question, let's return to our lesson, to listen for the word that it would mediate to each one of us here this morning.

Note, first of all, that the Apostle will not let us stop merely with the assertion that, because Jesus is the ascended Lord, the final power over all things is God's love and that it is this love that confronts each and every human being as gift and demand. No, his last word is not only that God has subjected all things to Christ, to the power of God's love, but that this same Christ, this same word to us of God's boundless love, is the supreme head of the church. Indeed, the Apostle goes so far as to say that this church, as the body of which Christ is the head, is "the fullness of him who fills all in all," is his own fullness, without which he himself would not be complete. This is apt to strike us as a strange thing to say, especially if we understand the whole last verse of the lesson as the early church fathers generally understood it. Recognizing that the Greek verb in this last sentence is, in fact, in the passive voice, they took it to mean, not, as our New Revised Standard Version has it, that Christ is the one "who fills all in all," but that he is the one "who is *being filled by* everything." And yet, strange or not, the meaning, I think, is quite clear: although Christ, and Christ alone, is the head of the church, the church is itself his body, without whose life in the world under his headship—under the gift and demand of God's love—he himself is not complete.

66

The word we're to hear in our lesson, then, is that we as Christians, as members of this congregation, are to be the community of God's love in our time and place: the community that, in confessing its faith in Christ's ascension into heaven, is to be the very body of Christ, the very fullness of God's love in the world. But if this is the word we're to hear, we should have no trouble understanding the Apostle's challenge to his readers to achieve an existential knowledge of God's love as a challenge addressed also to us. For the only knowledge of God that frees us to love is just such a knowledge of God's love for us: a knowledge in our hearts as well as our heads, the fruit of which is the loving service of our neighbors as ourselves through which we alone can be Christ's church.

Nor can such existential knowledge and love ever be something merely general and abstract. If the ascension of Christ is to be more than a mere belief *that* something, because it is genuinely a belief *in* some-one—in the all-sovereign God, and hence trust in that God's love and loyalty to its cause—it must always find quite specific and concrete ex-pression in all that we ourselves think, say, and do.

Only this week, *Time* magazine called attention to certain develop-ments in our city, of which only the relatively few readers of *The Texas Observer* had previously received any published report. It seems that the Dallas County Attorney's Office has issued certain instructions on "Jury Selection in a Criminal Case," which were written, interestingly enough, by the Assistant District Attorney who has the distinction of having se-cured the first 1,000-year sentence ever passed by a court in our city. Among the published excerpts from these instructions, one finds the following:

> You are not looking for a fair juror, but rather a strong, biased and sometimes hypocritical individual who believes that de-fendants are different in kind, rather than degree. You are not looking for any member of a minority group—they almost al-ways empathize with the accused. You are not looking for the freethinkers and flower children.
>
> Look for physical afflictions. These people usually empa-thize with the accused.
>
> I don't like women jurors because I can't trust them. They do, however, make the best jurors in cases involving crimes against children. It is possible that their 'women's intuition' can help you if you can't win your case with the facts.

> One who does not wear a coat and tie is often a noncon-
> formist and therefore a bad state's juror. Conservatively well-
> dressed people are generally stable and good for the state.

Now, my dear brothers and sisters, make no mistake about it: what
is said in these instructions to criminal prosecutors in our own community is itself a crime of lèse-majesté against the Lordship of Jesus
Christ that is witnessed to us on this Ascension Sunday. With a frankness
that is as callous as it is astonishing, those whom we entrust with the
responsibility of securing justice and fairness and equality before the law
are deliberately instructed to betray their public trust. But, offensive as
this is simply to ordinary legality and morality, it's intolerable from the
standpoint of Christian faith in Jesus Christ. For the demand for justice
is always a demand of love itself, and thus to counsel injustice is simply
to deny the word of Christ that the only all-sovereign power is the power
of God's love.

There are no two ways about it: one test of our faith in Christ's ascension into heaven, if it is to be a truly existential faith, is to bear witness
to his Lordship against this quite specific and concrete evil: to label it
for what it is, to speak out against it, to mobilize whatever forces may be
necessary to correct it, and, above all, to root out in ourselves and in our
fellow-citizens the kinds of attitudes and prejudices, the irrational fears
and anxieties, that alone give such instructions any purchase. After all,
most of us here, in this congregation, live right in the middle of those
"conservatively well-dressed people" who "are generally stable and good
for the state"; and it's only in this quite specific and concrete context that
we can be the community of God's love through Jesus Christ, and thus
live out our faith in our ascended Lord.

We've long been accustomed in this community to using an affirmation and a response by which we regularly bear witness to this basic
Christian faith. Of course, the affirmation we usually make and respond
to is, "The Lord is risen!" But not the least important thing to remember
on this Ascension Sunday is that, from New Testament times onward, it
is one and the same Christian faith that has found expression, whether
Christians affirmed Christ's resurrection-exaltation or his ascension into
heaven instead. I haven't the least hesitation, therefore, in summing up
all that I believe we are to hear this morning in those words that are so
familiar to us all—only I remind you in doing so of the challenge that
each of us in fact accepts in making them her or his own: "The Lord is
risen! *The Lord is risen, indeed!*" Amen.

2 December 1973

Ecclesiastes 9:7–10; 4:9–12

Go, eat your bread with enjoyment, and drink your wine with a merry heart; for God has long ago approved what you do. Let your garments always be white; do not let oil be lacking on your head. Enjoy life with the spouse whom you love, all the days of your vain life that are given you under the sun, because that is your portion in life and in your toil at which you toil under the sun. Whatever your hand finds to do, do with your might; for there is no work or thought or knowledge or wisdom in Sheol, to which you are going.

Two are better than one, because they have a good reward for their toil. For if they fall, one will lift up the other; but woe to one who is alone and falls and does not have another to help. Again, if two lie together, they keep warm; but how can one keep warm alone? And though one might prevail against another, two will withstand one. A threefold cord is not quickly broken.

Taken simply in themselves, as we've just heard them read, these words from Ecclesiastes, especially the last, may seem to involve an immediate and obvious reference to marriage. But the plain truth is that, in their original context, these words make no particular reference to marriage. Indeed, it's likely that, when one sets them in their context, they will seem to many of us to have no relevance to marriage at all.

That context, very briefly, is a series of reflections on the utter vanity of human existence. "Vanity of vanities"—that's the verdict that Ecclesiastes pronounces on human life. In this connection, he is led to reflect on the oppression of human beings by one another, at the same time recognizing in all honesty that, if they work together, they can to some

69

extent lighten their common burden. Thus two persons working together reap a larger reward from their toil because, by helping one another up when they fall, they can get more done. Or, again, two travelers lying together along the road on a cold Palestinian night can keep warmer than one lying alone. Or, yet again, two persons banded together are better able to withstand the attack of the robber—and if two banded together is good, three is even better (which seems to be the original meaning of the strange saying, "a threefold cord is not quickly broken").

The reference of the passage in context, then, is in no way to marriage, but simply to the values of cooperation in the struggle for existence that is our human lot. Its real point is epitomized in a single saying from the Talmud: "Either companionship or death."

But, although our passage, rightly understood, intends no reference to marriage, my conviction is that it is nevertheless profoundly relevant to the meaning of the relationship that we're gathered here this evening to solemnize. For what is it, finally, that marriage is all about?

Well, without a doubt, it's about the affection of man and woman for one another and the unique kind of relationship that such affection makes possible. It springs from the erotic love of man for woman and of woman for man; and if it is to be a good marriage, it must continue to be nourished by that kind of love. But, although erotic love is indeed necessary to marriage, it's another question whether it's also sufficient. In fact, it takes no great insight to discern from the traditional service of marriage that we're conducting here that something else—something very different—is also required. What the couple are asked to vow to one another is not a constancy in their mutual erotic attraction but a fidelity in their mutual relationship as persons: "for better, for worse, for richer, for poorer, in sickness and in health, . . . till death us do part."

In other words, marriage, finally, is intended to be precisely human companionship in bearing the burdens of life and in experiencing its joys. It is a real and true marriage only where each partner can look to the other in the confidence that there is at least one person in the world from whom he or she may expect security and warmth, comfort and protection: who will lift her up when she falls, will warm him against the chill of the night, and will stand with her against the onslaughts of the enemy.

In this sense, marriage is indeed a sacrament: a sacrament of the human companionship to which all of us are called and of that infinitely more than human companionship that is the deepest meaning of all our life with one another. Amen.

1 Corinthians 15:58

Therefore, my beloved, be steadfast, immovable, always excelling in the work of the Lord, because you know that in the Lord your labor is not in vain.

If my own experience is any indication, there's not much doubt about the deeper impact of the event of death, such as has brought all of us here together for this memorial service. Underlying all the grief we feel at another's passing and our keen sense that all our lives are thereby diminished, there's the even keener sense that we, too, each of us and all of us, are born to die. "On us and all our race the slow, sure doom falls pitiless and dark."

Of course, we've always known this somehow as long as we've known anything, and at the merely intellectual level we could have always told anyone who asked us that, all women and men being mortal, we, too, were bound to die. But one of the things the actual death of another can teach us is that, at a deeper level, we have also always tried to forget the fact of our own mortality, even though it forces itself upon us again and again. Otherwise, why should the event of death strike us with the force of a reminder—a reminder of our own radical contingency and transience in a radically contingent and transient world?

But it is to just such persons as ourselves, who've been newly reminded by death both of their own mortality and of their repeated sinful attempts to forget it, that the New Testament lessons we've heard are all addressed. Directly or indirectly, they all proclaim one and the same gospel of the love of God through Jesus Christ; and this gospel everywhere rests on one and the same presupposition. It presupposes that those for whom it is intended are women and men who know full well they're going to die but still have not come to terms with that fact; who, trying ever so desperately to forget their contingency and transience, again and again seek life in themselves and their world, only to fall ever more surely under the dominion of death. Precisely in trying to live, finally, from what they themselves are and have and do, they make death itself into a final power. For this reason, Paul can say elsewhere that the sting of death is sin, even as the wages of sin is death (1 Cor 15:56; Rom 6:23).

Yet it's to just such persons—and that means, as I've said, to just such sinners as ourselves—that our lessons all proclaim the forgiveness of sin and the overcoming of death. This they do because they all proclaim, in effect, that neither our life nor our death, nor even our sinful attempts to forget our death, has the kind of finality that we are inclined to suppose. Encompassing them all is that still more ultimate power whence all things come and whither they all go that reveals itself to us decisively through Jesus Christ as the power of boundless love. Because it is in this love that we are all freely given to share, we have no need to forget our own mortality and to try vainly to find life finally in ourselves. Instead, fully accepting our contingency and transience, we can look to God's love alone as our ultimate ground and end. Thus we hear from Peter that by God's great mercy through Christ we've been born anew into a living hope (1 Pet 1:3); and Paul assures us that, Christ being Lord both of the dead and of the living, neither death nor life, nor anything else in all creation will be able to separate us from the love of God that is ours through him (Rom 14:9; 8:38–39).

But it is the last of our New Testament lessons on which I would especially focus our attention, that is, on Paul's word to the Christians in Corinth, "Therefore, my beloved brothers and sisters, be steadfast, immovable, always excelling in the work of the Lord, because you know that in the Lord your labor is not in vain." This lesson stands out not only because it is expressly a word of address, but also because, being an imperative that directly calls for a response from the reader, it proclaims the gospel itself only indirectly. "Therefore," Paul begins, making clear in doing so that he is not so much proclaiming the gospel as presupposing it—in order, then, to draw the conclusion, or, better, to summon his reader to draw the conclusion, for which the gospel of God's love is the warrant. Because it is nothing other than this love that is the mystery encompassing our life, and because it is this love that is freely offered to each and every one of us decisively through Jesus Christ, therefore we can and should be steadfast and immovable even in the face of death. And that means, as Paul then goes on to explain, that we are to be ever more deeply engaged in the Lord's work, knowing in so doing that whatever we do, being done quite literally in the Lord, and therefore within God's own all-encompassing life, can never be done in vain but always fully counts and is of everlasting significance.

But, of course, Paul doesn't draw the conclusion in this indicative way; and if we would hear his word as also addressed to us, we must realize that he also doesn't say anything about the response that the gospel of God's love calls us to make. He simply summons each of us to make it—and to make it, moreover, in our very lives here and now by what we ourselves most immediately know and do.

And the real force of Paul's word comes home to us when we recall that it was originally addressed to those who, like most of us, were already professing Christians, and who, therefore, had already responded to the preaching of the gospel and therefore already knew the truth it proclaims. Maybe we, too, are inclined to suppose that we already know this truth simply because at the merely intellectual level we could tell anyone who asked us that this is what we as Christians believe and proclaim. But if this is so, Paul's word is here to tell us that we're deceived, because the knowledge of God's love, and so of the abiding significance of our own lives in God's life, is not a knowledge that we can ever simply have but, exactly like the more than intellectual knowledge of our own mortality, must be acquired ever and again anew in our most immediate understanding of our own existence. And this is the reason, of course, why the knowing to which Paul would summon us is entirely of a piece with doing, with what he means by "always excelling in the work of the Lord." To know God's love as the gospel summons each of us to know it is all tied up with doing the Lord's work: the work of building up the church—not, naturally, for the sake of the church, but always so as the better to enable the church to carry out that ministry of reconciliation that God, through Christ, has given to each and every one of us as the church, for the sake of the whole world (cf. 2 Cor 5:18–19).

It is so like our dear brother to have given careful thought to what should be said and sung in this service and to have left explicit instructions that any preaching in it should not be talk about him, but solely and simply proclaiming the gospel. I should like to think that, in trying to preach the gospel as it addresses us especially in this word of Paul's,

I have carried out his instructions. And yet I must now confess to you quite openly that it is, above all, my unforgettable impression of him himself—of what he did and was just as much as of what he said and wrote—that has constrained me to focus our attention especially on this lesson. Indeed, I can only believe that I shall always see him with the eye of my mind and heart as one who, in all the limitations of his humanity, was a veritable proclamation of this apostolic word. To each of us who knew him he was an ever-renewed summons to draw the conclusion in our own life here and now of God's boundless love for us through Christ Jesus our Lord—and, therefore, to be steadfast and immovable, always excelling in the work of the Lord, knowing that, in the Lord, our labor is not in vain. Amen.

1 *Peter* 1:13–25

Therefore prepare your minds for action; discipline yourselves; set all your hope on the grace that Jesus Christ will bring you when he is revealed. Like obedient children, do not be conformed to the desires that you formerly had in ignorance. Instead, as he who called you is holy, be holy yourselves in all your conduct; for it is written, "You shall be holy, for I am holy."

If you invoke as Father the one who judges all people impartially according to their deeds, live in reverent fear during the time of your exile. You know that you were ransomed from the futile ways inherited from your ancestors, not with perishable things like silver or gold, but with the precious blood of Christ, like that of a lamb without defect or blemish. He was destined before the foundation of the world, but was revealed at the end of the ages for your sake. Through him you have come to trust in God, who raised him from the dead and gave him glory, so that your faith and hope are set on God.

Now that you have purified your souls by your obedience to the truth so that you have genuine mutual love, love one another deeply from the heart. You have been born anew, not of perishable but of imperishable seed, through the living and enduring word of God. For

> *"All flesh is grass*
> *and all its glory like the flower of grass.*
> *The grass withers,*
> *and the flower falls,*
> *but the word of the Lord endures forever."*

That word is the good news that was announced to you.

Scholars today seem generally agreed that the lesson we've just heard read—which one of them aptly characterizes as an "admonition to holy living"—has its immediate context in what appears to have been an address to newly baptized Christians. This, at any rate, seems to have been the original purpose of that larger part of 1 Peter to which our lesson immediately belongs, even if it was subsequently made to serve a somewhat different purpose by the addition of the smaller part comprising the opening two verses and everything in the fourth and fifth chapters from v. 11 of chapter 4 on. The setting in the life of the church evidently reflected in this later beginning and ending of the letter as we now have it was one in which the church was passing through the fiery ordeal of persecution, and therefore was in peculiar need of the strength to endure and to hold fast to its faith. Thus what was originally a baptismal address became, in effect, a baptismal remembrance, the aim of which was to encourage Christians to stand firm in their trials by reminding them of the meaning of their baptism.

But in whichever of these contexts we take it, whether as address or as remembrance, our lesson presumably has something directly to say to us today. Whether we ourselves are new Christians or old, our situation remains essentially the same, insofar as we are ever confronted by the same gift and demand of God through Christ as they are re-presented to each of us individually in the indicatives and imperatives of our own baptism. Moreover, there is merely a difference in degree, in no way a difference in kind, between the familiar trials and temptations of day-to-day Christian existence and the extreme trials and tribulations of out-and-out persecution. In the one situation as much as in the other, faith must be realized again and again anew in face of the concrete option of unfaith; and if there is any encouragement in either situation sufficient to enable us to withstand that option, it lies solely in God's prevenient love for us decisively through Christ, of which our baptism ever remains the concrete symbol.

Of course, the relevance of our lesson to our own situation here and now in no way implies that we would, or even could, make use of its concepts and terms in order to bear witness to our own Christian faith today. On the contrary, the more we struggle to grasp the meaning of our lesson in either of the contexts in which we might try to understand it, the clearer it must become to us that, for all of the similarity between the situation of those to whom it was originally addressed and our own, it is only in concepts and terms very different from theirs that we are able to think and speak. As a matter of fact, this is apt to strike us with particular force when we come to the assertions about God and Christ that are, as it were, the hinge on which the lesson turns.

I speak of these assertions as the hinge of our lesson because, clearly, the several imperatives that give it its character as an admonition are all based on the indicatives that these assertions express. "Therefore," it begins, "prepare your minds for action; discipline yourselves; set all your hope on the grace that Jesus Christ will bring you when he is revealed." Clearly, this demand to get our thoughts together, to keep our eyes open, and to hope solely in the coming grace of God makes no sense unless the assertion is true that the final end of all things, and thus what is coming to each of us out of the future is the grace of God decisively revealed through Jesus Christ. Similarly, the reason we ourselves are to be holy in all our conduct is that the God who has called us is holy; and we are to conduct ourselves with fear throughout the time of our earthly exile because it is precisely this holy God whom we have now been taught to call our Father, and who, being no respecter of persons, judges each of us impartially according to our deeds.

The same thing may be said of the christological assertions that we find at the very center of our lesson. "You know that you were ransomed from the futile ways inherited from your ancestors, not with perishable things like silver or gold, but with the precious blood of Christ, like that of a lamb without defect or blemish. He was destined before the foundation of the world, but was revealed at the end of the ages for your sake. Through him you have come to trust in God, who raised him from the dead and gave him glory, so that your faith and hope are set on God." Without a doubt, it is the indicatives expressed by these central christological assertions that provide the basis for all the imperatives in our lesson. Because it is God who has decisively acted for us through the event of Christ, we not only can but also should understand ourselves and the world in the radically new way of all whose faith and hope are in that same God. And yet, every bit as certain is that it is above all in these very christological assertions, whose main point is to assert exactly this, that we are most struck by a whole way of thinking and speaking that we today find completely alien. Here, in fact, is what has been called "the myth of God incarnate" with a vengeance, and, if we are at all honest with ourselves, we know that we can appropriate the witness that our lesson would bear to us only insofar as we can demythologize it.

But honesty also compels us to admit that there are always dangers in demythologizing that past experience has shown to be serious. Nor is there the least reason to suppose that we today are at last safe against such dangers. On the contrary, in the recent discussion, to whose title I have just alluded, most of the participants seem to take the position that what the myth of God's incarnation in Christ is properly understood to express is the significance of the one believer, Jesus of Nazareth, for all the rest of us who are called to believe in God. Thus, on this position, Jesus is—as one discussant puts it—"our sufficient model of true humanity in a perfect relationship to God. And he is so far above us in the 'direction' of God that he stands between ourselves and the Ultimate as a mediator of salvation." As convinced as I am that the myth of God incarnate must indeed be demythologized, I'm just as convinced that this is not the way to demythologize it—not, at any rate, if we're at all concerned to be faithful to what the New Testament intends to assert by means of it. For the Jesus whom the New Testament writings overwhelmingly assert to be the Christ is much less a sufficient example of human faith than he is the primal sacrament of divine grace. This is why they typically represent him to us, not merely as the one *with* whom we are to believe in God, but rather as the one decisively *through* whom we are to believe—as himself the real presence to us and to all other women and men who will receive him of the gift and demand of God's own prevenient love for the world.

And this, of course, is just the kind of christology that addresses us in our lesson. In asserting that Christ was destined before the foundation of the world, even though he was revealed only at the end of the ages for our sake, our lesson intends to say simply that what decisively encounters us through Jesus Christ, by means of the church's word of preaching and its sacraments, is nothing other or less than God's own gift and demand. As such, they are and must be before the foundation of this world just as of any other world that is so much as possible. That this is so is fully confirmed when the lesson proceeds to assert that what is ours through Christ is trust in God, the God who raised Christ from the dead and gave him glory, so that our faith and hope would be set on nothing besides this one and only God. Here, by means of the plainly mythological talk of Christ's resurrection and glorification, identically the same point is made as by the equally mythological assertions of his pre-existence and incarnation—namely, that, as Paul puts it in a very similar context, "all this is from God" (2 Cor 5:18). What we really have to do with in Jesus Christ is not just another human being who is somewhere above us in the direction of God but the real presence here and now among us of God Godself—of that God whose boundless love for us and for all is not just the sole primal source of all things, and of our own being and meaning, but no less surely their and our sole final end.

But this is not all our lesson can teach us. We can also learn from it why the question of the kind of christology we have is far from a merely intellectual question of no existential importance. Consider what it goes on to say: "Now that you have purified your souls by your obedience to the truth so that you have genuine mutual love, love one another deeply from the heart. You have been born anew, not of perishable but of imperishable seed, through the living and enduring word of God . . . That word is the good news that was announced to you." In other words, the whole end of the faith that is "obedience to the truth" is such a radical transformation of our own existence as makes possible our genuinely loving any and all of our brothers and sisters. But the lesson also makes clear that it can admonish us thus to love one another genuinely and deeply just because—though, clearly, *only* because—we have in fact undergone such a radical transformation. "You have been born anew," it assures us, "not of perishable but of imperishable seed," which is to say, not of a human being but of God. What has encountered each of us through the church's preaching and sacraments is not just the word of human beings, but also "the living and enduring word of God." The ground of this divine word, however, and its only sufficient ground, cannot be merely another human being like ourselves, however far above us, but can only be the one human being through whom God Godself is decisively re-presented to us as the gift and demand of boundless love. Nothing other or less than God's own unbounded love for us can make possible our own love for one another "deeply from the heart." For only by the radical transformation of new birth can we thus love one another, and it is by God's love alone, obediently accepted through faith, that any of us has been born anew.

What is at stake in the question of christology, then, is nothing less than our own possibility precisely as Christians of existing in faith and hope in God and in a deep, genuine love of one another. This, too, our lesson can teach us, even while we can learn from its own christological assertions, as mythological as they certainly are, the one essential truth to which any christology worth the name must somehow bear witness.

At the same time, our lesson itself makes clear that the whole end of our obedience to the truth of christology, and hence the whole point of christology itself, is precisely a deep, genuine love of all our brothers and sisters. Therefore, if it is our own possibility of existing as Christians that requires us somehow to bear witness to "the truth of God incarnate," it is not only, or even primarily, by our christology, by what we explicitly think and say about Christ, that we are to bear witness to this truth. No, our primary witness to the truth of God's real presence among us decisively through Jesus is our deep, genuine love of one another. And it includes, among other things, the kind of pastoral concern that is sensitive to the difficulties that others may well have with the mythological assertions of traditional christology even if we ourselves do not.

Of course, if we're really concerned about others, foremost among the things we'll want to share with them is the truth about Christ as we've been given to understand it. Moreover, we will be at pains to make clear to them that not just any christology is able to take account of this truth at all adequately. But the fact remains that it is primarily by actually living for others out of a deep, genuine love for them, and thus by seeking to respond to all of their human needs, that we really hear and believe the witness of our lesson. It is above all by living this kind of a loving life, and not by what we think or say, however rightly, about its ground, that we fulfill the imperatives and thereby bear witness to the indicatives of our own baptism. Amen.

Matthew 15:21–28

Jesus left that place and went away to the district of Tyre and Sidon. Just then a Canaanite woman from that region came out and started shouting. "Have mercy on me, Lord, Son of David; my daughter is tormented by a demon." But he did not answer her at all. And his disciples came and urged him, saying, "Send her away, for she keeps shouting after us." He answered, "I was sent only to the lost sheep of the house of Israel." But she came and knelt before him, saying, "Lord, help me." He answered, "It is not fair to take the children's food and throw it to the dogs." She said, "Yes, Lord, yet even the dogs eat the crumbs that fall from their master's table." Then Jesus answered her, "Woman great is your faith! Let it be done for you as you wish." And her daughter was healed instantly.

Our Gospel lesson this morning has been traditionally appointed for the Second Sunday in Lent. Concerned, as it appears to be, with Jesus' exorcism of the possessed daughter of the Canaanite woman, it was once taken to have a particular relevance to that season of the church year when, along with their instruction in Christian faith, those who were to be baptized at Easter themselves engaged in fasting directed toward exorcising demons. But from the standpoint of contemporary gospel scholarship, this association of the lesson with Lent is dubious. In form, the story the lesson tells is not so much an exorcism or healing story as it is a saying story—although, unlike most such stories in the gospels, the saying for which it provides the setting is at least as much what is said by the woman as it is anything that Jesus says. As for its content, its real focus, like that of many of the other healing stories in the gospels, is not on

Jesus the exorcist of demons, but on Jesus the evoker of faith—with the singular difference that, in this story, the emphasis falls on the faith that he evokes and on the nature of such faith as it's represented concretely by the Canaanite woman.

Of course, the insight that the story really has to do with faith is not a discovery of modern historical scholarship. Luther's sermons on our lesson, for instance, are penetrating analyses of the nature of the faith that, in spite of all obstacles and temptations, clings to the word that evokes it. But, for all of its penetration and power, even Luther's way of understanding the lesson is hard to square with what critical historical scholarship now teaches us concerning it.

The question, therefore, is whether the story our lesson tells still has something to say to us, even when we take seriously all that we've now been taught about its form and content as well as its larger context and use. Since the real content of the story is the nature of faith, we need to ask whether it has anything to say to us today to deepen our understanding of Christian faith and to make us more thoughtful about ourselves in relation to it.

I

We begin to glimpse an answer, I believe, as soon as we recognize the larger context and use of the story in Matthew's Gospel. As I had occasion to realize not too long ago, from a conversation with a man who had for the first time undertaken to read them carefully, readers of the gospels are still sometimes shocked to discover that Jesus evidently restricted his mission to his own people. Yet this is how all the gospels take Jesus to have understood his mission when they represent him as saying, in the words of our lesson, "I was sent only to the lost sheep of the house of Israel." And this is nowhere expressed more clearly than in the Gospel according to Matthew generally and in our lesson in particular, where Jesus' limitation of his mission to Israel is so emphatic as to have led the man with whom I spoke to be put off by what he called, "Jesus' ethnocentrism." "It is not fair," Jesus is made to say, "to take the children's food and throw it to the dogs."

To be sure, it's also in Matthew's Gospel that we find the risen Jesus issuing the so-called great commission: "Go therefore and make disciples of all nations, baptizing them in the name of the Father and of the Son and of the Holy Spirit, and teaching them to obey everything that I have commanded you" (28:19–20). But Matthew is quite clear that this is the new and different commission precisely of the risen Jesus; and we know from his allegorical interpretation of the Parable of the Wedding Banquet in chapter 22 that he understood God to have summoned the gentiles into the kingdom only after the Jews had rejected God's invitation when it had come to them earlier through the prophets and the apostles.

At the same time, Matthew is enough of a champion of the church's mission to the gentiles to have an interest in its having already been anticipated during Jesus' own ministry. And so he includes in his Gospel not only the story that makes up our lesson, but also the only other story in the entire gospel-tradition in which a gentile is represented as accepting Jesus' call to faith—namely, the story of the healing of the servant of the centurion at Capernaum in chapter 8. In both stories, which are quite similar in form and also in content, the focus of interest is not on the healing that Jesus performs, but on the faith that Jesus evokes—precisely from a gentile to whom his call to faith is not even addressed! In sharp contrast to the believing Jews who reject his call, the Canaanite woman and the Roman centurion, although mere unbelieving gentiles, are so strong in their faith as to claim his gift of salvation. "Woman great is your faith! Let it be done for you as you wish." Or, as Jesus says in the other story of the centurion, "Truly I tell you, in no one in Israel have I found such faith . . . . Go; let it be done for you according to your faith." Significantly, Matthew adds to these words a saying of Jesus that denies all security to those who belong to the believing community of Israel. "I tell you, many will come from east and west and will eat with Abraham and Isaac and Jacob in the kingdom of heaven, while the heirs of the kingdom will be thrown into the outer darkness" (8:10–12).

There is no question, then, about the use to which Matthew puts our story in the larger context of his Gospel. Along with the closely parallel story of the centurion at Capernaum, the story of the Canaanite woman serves to point up the contrast between two very different responses to Jesus' call to faith: on the one hand, the rejection of his call by the believing community to whom he is sent; on the other hand, the acceptance of his call by unbelieving individuals to whom he himself does not even recognize a mission.

III

But now what does any of this have to say to you and me?

Granted that the faith of the Canaanite woman contrasts sharply with the rejection of Jesus' call by all but a few of his own people, what can recognizing this do today beyond feeding a kind of Christian triumphalism and a false sense of security on the part of us who call ourselves Christians? After all, there is scarcely a one of us who is not an heir or heiress of the mission to the gentiles, which is anticipated in this story of the Canaanite woman's faith. Unlike the Jews who rejected Jesus' mission, our forebears were, for the most part, gentiles who accepted it. In purely historical terms, then, we are the sons and daughters, not of unbelieving Jews, but of believing gentiles—of those who, like the woman in our story, responded to Jesus' call with faith and thus claimed the salvation that he has the power to give.

So we are—in purely historical terms. But why should we suppose that they are the only, or even the primary, terms in which we are to understand ourselves and our lesson? Nothing is clearer to anyone who carefully studies the gospels and understands the purpose for which they're written than that they are far from being intended merely, or even primarily, as historical accounts. Right from the beginning of the gospel-tradition, the primary, if not the only, purpose of all the stories and sayings that we find in the gospels is to bear witness to Jesus as the Christ: as the anointed one of God through whom God's own call to faith is finally and decisively issued to all humankind. Nor can there be any question that this is also the controlling purpose of the gospels themselves, including the Gospel from which our lesson is taken. If Matthew contrasts, as he does, the faith of certain gentiles with the unfaith of the Jews, he is not making a merely historical statement, nor does he have the least intention, finally, of nourishing Christian triumphalism and a false sense of security on the part of those for whom his Gospel is written. In fact, we have every good reason in our lesson itself to identify ourselves as Christians today, not with the Canaanite woman who accepted Jesus' call to faith, but with his own people who, for the most part, rejected it.

And this identification becomes all the more clearly indicated, the more we understand the real nature of Christian faith. Contrary to what it is often thought to be, such faith is, first of all, faith or *belief in* Jesus, in his call to faith as God's own call also to us, not merely certain *beliefs about* Jesus. In other words, Christian faith is not primarily assent to the

Christian world view, in the sense of the system of beliefs about Jesus himself as well as about ourselves, the world, and God in which faith in Jesus' call has historically found expression. Rather, faith is always, first and last, trust in Jesus' call itself—trust in it, namely, as God's own call to each of us to entrust ourselves utterly and completely to God's boundless love for us as the only final meaning of our life. This means that faith in the primary sense of the word is never a decision we already have behind us but is ever a decision we still have ahead of us. We can have such faith, and in that sense *be* Christians, only by ever and again coming to such faith, so as thereby to *become* Christians.

Of course, anyone who assents to Christian beliefs as true in some sense has Christian faith and is insofar a Christian as she or he thereby belongs to the visible Christian church. But belonging to the visible church is one thing, belonging to the invisible community of those who trust in God's call in every new present, something else. And what is primarily meant by Christian faith is always and only the second of these things. It is the ever-new act of trust out of the depth of one's own need, and regardless of one's beliefs or lack of beliefs, in the call of Jesus as the loving call of God Godself.

Once we recognize this, however, it should be clear why we can rightly understand our lesson only if we put ourselves in the position, not of the Canaanite woman, or even of the disciples, but of those who are spoken of in the story as the house of Israel. For, so far as our being Christian is something already decided in the past, we are in no different position from the people of Israel to whom Jesus understood himself to be sent. This is obvious enough from the fact that we, too, have our ways of distinguishing between the sheep in our house who are saved and the other sheep who are lost. And those of us who are wont to reckon ourselves among the saved are clearly just as likely as the Jews ever were to miss the point of Jesus' words that it is only to the lost sheep of the house of Israel that he is sent. For we, too, can imagine that being saved or lost is something already decided by what we ourselves have or are by our Christian beliefs, instead of something that must ever be decided anew in face of Jesus' call to faith—a call through which even the saved are again and again given to discover their lostness.

To be sure, our system of beliefs as Christians is different—not least because it includes certain beliefs about Jesus himself that Jewish beliefs do not include. But with respect to the crucial question of faith, of Jesus' call to faith and of our own acceptance or rejection of it, we are in exactly the same position as the Jews of his own day. For this call one must accept not only with the knowledge and assent of one's mind, but also with the trust and loyalty of one's heart; and this means that one must accept it ever and again anew out of the depth of one's own need simply as a human being.

It is precisely our own faith as Christians, then, that we are to judge by the faith of the Canaanite woman. Consider her situation. On the most obvious level, she is a Canaanite, and that means, of course, one who lacks the beliefs of the Jews, and so does not belong to the visible community of Israel to which Jesus is presented as understanding himself to be sent. Whatever the religious beliefs through which she is accustomed to understand herself—and about this the lesson is completely silent—they clearly are not the historic Jewish beliefs in terms of which Jesus' call to faith is issued—just as there are many persons with whom we live today who do not understand themselves in terms of our historic beliefs as Christians. But, at a deeper level, the Canaanite woman is simply a woman—more exactly, a mother, who has assumed responsibility for the daughter for whose healing she is so concerned. Whatever her religious beliefs, if, indeed, she even has any, she's fully engaged in trying to be and to become a human being by loving the one whom she has been given to love—just as there are those today outside the visible church who are fully engaged in the work of love, often with a seriousness and dedication that put our own lack of love for others to shame. But the course of such love never runs smooth, and it always has its limits. There is just so much that any human love can do, and in the case of this woman the limit of love is the demon possessing her daughter—just as in our world today the most intractable limits of love are the truly demonic structures of injustice and oppression that thwart the lives of those for whom we are responsible. At its depth, then, the situation of the Canaanite woman is simply that of a human being who loves but whose own love is finally powerless to save. And it is out of this situation of profound human need that she responds to what she's heard about Jesus with a faith that simply won't take No for an answer.

The word of our lesson to us, then, is that it is out of this kind of a human situation—and, finally, only out of it—that we, too, must respond to Jesus' call if we're really to respond in faith. Unless and until our Christian faith is something to which we are literally driven by our own profound need for help—for a power greater than our own, a divine love that can save even when we're powerless to save—it cannot be the faith to which Jesus calls us. For he does not call us merely to accept certain religious beliefs but to trust in his word as God's own word of love for us and for all our fellow men and women. And such trust is not even possible unless and until we feel our own profound need for it—unless and until we realize that, for all of our obvious difference from those who do not share our Christian beliefs, we are at bottom one with them in our abiding dependence on God's love as the only power that can finally help us.

Yet, if we're to realize this, we, too, must be fully engaged in the work of love in the world, in loyally serving and caring for all whom we have been given to love. For only if we love can we experience the inevitable limits of human love, and thus feel the need for the divine love in which Jesus calls us to trust with all our hearts.

"Lord, help me," the woman finally begs on her knees. And when Jesus responds that it is not fair to take the children's food and throw it to the dogs, she says, simply, "Yes, Lord, yet even the dogs eat the crumbs that fall from their master's table." Such is the faith by which we're to judge our own Christian faith. For our faith is truly Christian only when, even as children, our felt need to be fed from our Father's table remains as great as the dogs'. But, then, if our faith in God's love is as great as our need for it, we, too, may hear Jesus' words, "Great is your faith! Let it be done for you as you wish." Amen.

John 2:1–12

On the third day there was a wedding in Cana of Galilee, and the mother of Jesus was there. Jesus and his disciples had also been invited to the wedding. When the wine gave out, the mother of Jesus said to him, "They have no wine." And Jesus said to her, "Woman, what concern is that to you and to me? My hour has not yet come." His mother said to the servants, "Do whatever he tells you." Now standing there were six stone water jars for the Jewish rites of purification, each holding twenty or thirty gallons. Jesus said to them, "Fill the jars with water." And they filled them up to the brim. He said to them, "Now draw some out, and take it to the chief steward." So they took it. When the steward tasted the water that had become wine, and did not know where it came from (though the servants who had drawn the water knew), the steward called the bridegroom and said to him, "Everyone serves the good wine first, and then the inferior wine after the guests have become drunk. But you have kept the good wine until now." Jesus did this, the first of his signs, in Cana of Galilee, and revealed his glory; and his disciples believed in him.

After this he went down to Capernaum with his mother, his brothers, and his disciples; and they remained there a few days.

Our Gospel lesson this morning is the story of a miracle that it itself designates as the first of Jesus' signs. This designation is important because of the clue it gives us as to the meaning of the story in the larger context of the Gospel according to John. At the end of chapter 20, just after the risen Jesus has met and overcome Thomas' unbelief, the reader is told, "Now Jesus did many other signs in the presence of his disciples, which are not written in this book. But these are written so that you may come to believe that Jesus is the Christ, the Son of God, and that through believing you may have life in his name" (vv. 30–31). It is presumably for this same reason that the story of the miracle at the wedding in Cana is also written. It, too, is included in the Gospel as a sign, whose purpose is to evoke that faith in Jesus as the Christ, the Son of God, that is truly life.

But just what does this mean to us? Are we to respond to our lesson by first believing that Jesus actually performed the miracle of turning water into wine and, then, because we believe this, also believe in his decisive significance for our lives?

Whatever may have been the case in the "signs source" that John appears to have made use of in writing his Gospel, this is not the response that he would have us make. For, as he presents it, this first of Jesus' signs, exactly like all the others, is clearly a symbol, in that it points beyond itself to something else. And this is so even if there is every reason to suppose that John himself believed that Jesus did in fact change the water into wine just as the story says he did.

That the meaning of our lesson is symbolic is clearly indicated by Jesus' response to his mother's report that there is no more wine for the wedding feast. "Woman, what concern is that to you and to me? My hour has not yet come." Even in form this response makes clear that Jesus' concern and his mother's are different, and this alone should keep us from supposing that, when Jesus goes on to change the water into wine, he is merely complying, however reluctantly, with what his mother wants him to do. But the content of his response makes this still clearer; for he says that his hour has not yet come; and, as any reader of John's Gospel knows, any talk of Jesus' hour throughout the Gospel refers unmistakably to his death and exaltation as the climactic moment in the whole event occurring through him. Thus Jesus responds to his mother by saying, in effect, that his concern, unlike hers, is not with providing wine for the wedding feast, but rather with the other, very different event of which his own passion and exaltation are the climax.

There is no question about what we're to understand by this other event with which Jesus is concerned if we take account of the context of our lesson in the Gospel as a whole. I could put it in my own terms by saying that it is the event of his so re-presenting the gift and demand of God's love that women and men are explicitly confronted with the possibility of faith. But the characteristic way in which John speaks of this event is to speak of Jesus revealing his glory to those who believe in him. For the glory of Jesus that John speaks of throughout the Gospel is not the glory of the miracle-worker but the glory of him who decisively re-presents the possibility of faith as he is seen by those who believe in him. Thus, in the well-known passage in the Prologue to the Gospel, where John confesses with his fellow believers, "And the Word became flesh and lived among us, and we have seen his glory, the glory as of a father's only son," he goes on to declare, "No one has ever seen God. It is God the only Son, who is close to the Father's heart, who has made him known" (1:14, 18). The glory of Jesus as of the only Son from the Father is the glory he reveals by making known the unseen God—just as, correspondingly, those who allow him to make this God known to them are those who believe in him and see his glory. And this, of course, is just why John can conceive the whole event of Jesus' re-presenting God as reaching its climax in the hour of his passion and exaltation and can speak of it, accordingly, as the hour of his glorification (12:23, 27; 13:31–32; 17:1). For if Jesus' death is the climactic moment in his re-presenting God, and so revealing his own glory as God's Revealer, the climactic moment of the disciples' accepting his re-presentation, and thus seeing his glory, is his resurrection.

But once we recognize this, the symbolic meaning of our lesson is obvious. For it itself says expressly, in speaking of Jesus' miracle, "Jesus did this, the first of his signs, in Cana of Galilee, and revealed his glory; and his disciples believed in him" (v. 11). There, in the words of our lesson itself, is the confirmation that the sign Jesus did is indeed a symbol, and thus not merely the miracle his mother wanted him to perform. For all that the miracle required was that Jesus turn water into wine, whereas the sign was really done only when he was experienced by his disciples as so re-presenting the gift and demand of God's love as to turn their old existence in sin into their new life of faith.

The response our lesson calls for, then, in no way requires that we first believe in a miracle that may or may not have happened. Whether we do or do not believe that Jesus changed the water into wine, the symbolic meaning of our lesson remains, and it still asks us to believe in Jesus as the one whom it attests him to be: not a mere worker of miracles, but the doer of signs, as the only Son from the Father whose glory we see just insofar as we're willing to receive through faith from the fullness of grace and truth that are given us through him.

But this is to say that the response called for by our lesson is the same response of faith that we must presently bring to the Lord's table if it is to be for us a real sacrament. Just as we will not first have to believe in the miracle of transubstantiation before we can discern the real presence of Christ in the elements of bread and wine, so we do not first have to believe in the miracle of changing water into wine before we can see the glory of Jesus to which our lesson bears witness. On the contrary, the faith that is called for in the one case just as in the other is the faith that the gift and demand of love that are decisively re-presented to us through Jesus are none other than the eternal Word of God's own love for us now made fully explicit.

May God grant us to respond with such faith to all of Jesus' signs— those that are written and those that he still does—so that believing that he is indeed the Christ, the Son of God, we, too, may have life in his name. Amen.

25 MAY 1980

John 20:19–23

When it was evening on that day, the first day of the week, and the doors of the house where the disciples had met were locked for fear of the Jews, Jesus came and stood among them and said, "Peace be with you." After he said this, he showed them his hands and his side. Then the disciples rejoiced when they saw the Lord. Jesus said to them again, "Peace be with you. As the Father has sent me, so I send you." When he had said this, he breathed on them and said to them, "Receive the Holy Spirit. If you forgive the sins of any, they are forgiven them; if you retain the sins of any, they are retained."

Those of you who are familiar with the Mexican history and culture that have contributed so much to shaping our life in the Southwest know of the importance of *el Cinco de Mayo*, the Fifth of May. A year or so ago, as I was driving home in the evening, I was listening, as I generally do, to "All Things Considered." Since the date was 5 May, the program featured an on-the-scene report from an celebration then in progress somewhere in California—Los Angeles, as I recall. Included in the report were several interviews with the Mexican-American college students who were evidently participating in the festivities with not a little enthusiasm. What the interviewer wanted to know was simply the reason for their celebration—what the event was that they were celebrating. The striking thing was that not one of them was really able to tell her—most of them admitting in so many words that celebrating on this date was simply an essential part of their ethnic heritage, with the implication that that was all the reason they needed in order to celebrate.

Now I can't imagine that the result would be quite the same if an interviewer were to put a similar question to those of us who are gathered here this morning to participate in another celebration—although I must say, in all frankness, that after some of the liturgical extravaganzas I've been a part of in recent years on Pentecost, I sometimes wonder whether the difference would really be as great as I would like to believe! Still, I have some confidence that most of us know why we're gathered for a special celebration this Sunday morning. At any rate, one of the essentials of our celebration, just as in traditional Pentecost celebrations generally, is the reading of lessons from the New Testament—especially the familiar lesson from the Acts of the Apostles (2:1–11)—that make clear to all of us what the event is that we're celebrating. Unless, then, we get so caught up in the inessentials of our celebration as to miss the reference of our lessons, none of us should be at all uncertain about why we're doing what we're doing. We're celebrating our own birthday as the church: the constituting event of the coming of the Holy Spirit through which the community of faith and witness of which we ourselves are members first came into being.

But just what all is involved in this event, and how, exactly, are we supposed to celebrate it?

Evidently there are important differences between it and an event such as the Battle of Puebla that *el Cinco de Mayo* commemorates. This is clear enough from our two lessons, which give different, even contradictory, accounts of the event of the Spirit's coming. In fact, they expressly disagree even about the date of the event—the lesson from John's Gospel explicitly affirming that it already took place on Easter evening, immediately following the appearance of the risen Jesus, while the lesson from Acts is just as explicit in assigning it to the day of Pentecost some fifty days later. What's more, if we locate our two lessons in their original contexts in the larger accounts of which they're respectively parts—the Gospel according to John, in the one case, and the two-volume work scholars now call Luke–Acts, in the other—we immediately notice a number of other discrepancies. Of course, interpreters have traditionally tried to avoid admitting this by harmonizing the two accounts—usually by arguing that Jesus' breathing of the Holy Spirit on the disciples on Easter evening was but an earnest or foretaste of the actual coming of the Spirit that took place only later, on the day of Pentecost. But we now know that any such harmonizing is completely unhistorical and seriously misleading as to the real meaning of the texts. The truth of the matter is that neither account was written with the other in mind but is an entirely independent witness to one and the same event; so there's nothing else to do but simply accept the fact of the discrepancies between them.

Once we do this, however, we can hardly suppose any longer that the purpose of either account was to provide a straightforward historical report of a past event. If that was their purpose, then the conclusion is inescapable that they failed to achieve it. But what was it, then, that these accounts were intended to do?

We begin to get an answer, I suggest, when we observe that, for all of the respects in which the two accounts are different, there are two important respects in which they're clearly the same: they both bear witness to the coming of the Holy Spirit to the first disciples; and they both understand this event of the Spirit's coming as constituting the church in its distinctive mission—the mission, namely, of continuing the mission of Jesus himself, who, having been lifted up on the cross, is now risen from the dead and exalted to his Father. Thus, according to the account in Acts, the coming of the Spirit so graphically depicted in our lesson is the fulfillment of Jesus' promise to the apostles attested in the preceding chapter: "This is what you have heard from me; for John baptized with water, but you will be baptized with the Holy Spirit not many days from now . . . You will receive power when the Holy Spirit has come upon you; and you will be my witnesses in Jerusalem, in all Judea and Samaria, and to the ends of the earth" (1:4–5, 8). And so, too, according to the other account in John's Gospel: "As the Father has sent me," Jesus says, "so I send you." Whereupon, breathing on the disciples, he says, "Receive the Holy Spirit. If you forgive the sins of any, they are forgiven them; if you retain the sins of any, they are retained." Just as Jesus has been given authority to execute the Father's judgment in the world, so now Jesus, in turn, gives the disciples the same divine authority (cf. 5:22–27). So much so, indeed, that he can assure them: "Very truly, I tell you, whoever receives one whom I send receives me; and whoever receives me receives him who sent me" (13:20).

The purpose of the two accounts, then, seems clear. So far from being intended simply to report a past historical event, they are, rather, witnesses of faith in the decisive significance of such an event. In their very different, even contradictory, ways, they're both intended, quite simply, to bear witness that the church is of God, that, notwithstanding the truly human nature both of the church itself and of the Jesus who sends it, the event of its coming into being is due to God's own loving action. Why? Well, because no one other or less than God Godself has authorized the mission both of Jesus and of the community of witnesses whom he in turn has appointed to continue it.

This is all made particularly clear by our lesson from John's Gospel, where, unlike our other lesson from Acts, the appearance of the risen Jesus and the coming of the Spirit that constitutes the church are presented together in their essential unity. It's important to underscore this because it's precisely their very different presentation in Luke-Acts, in which they are separated and presented as two entirely different events, that has determined the structure of our traditional church year and thereby shaped all of our theological understandings. The abiding value of John's presentation is to make clear that, in their essential meaning, Easter and Pentecost are not two events but one. The appearance of the risen Jesus to the first disciples and the coming of the Holy Spirit that constituted them the church are but two essential aspects of one and the same event: the church's coming into being as the church of Jesus Christ, through whose Spirit-inspired witness to him as the one sent by God his own mission in the world continues to take place.

All this, I say, is more than clear from our Gospel lesson. And yet not even it is sufficient to answer our question about what is involved in the event we're celebrating and what it means properly to celebrate it. For to say that the church is of God because the Jesus who sends the church has himself been sent from God is, in itself, to make a purely formal statement that is far from giving us a satisfactory answer to our question.

This will come home to you, I think, as soon as you reflect that talk about God is simply one of the ways in which we human beings have traditionally talked about the ultimate meaning of our own existence. The symbol-concept "God" properly functions in its ordinary religious uses to designate that mysterious and all-encompassing power that, being whatever it is, finally shapes whatever else may come to be, including whatever we ourselves may possibly become. This means, then, that the question that God-talk as such inevitably raises and tries to answer is just who or what this final, mysterious power really is and how we, accordingly, both can and should understand ourselves and the world in relation to it. But it also means that to say merely, as our lesson does, that the Jesus who sends the church has himself been sent by God is to say purely formally that Jesus and the church are, in their respective ways, of decisive significance for our existence without in any way saying materially what this actually means for us as regards our own possibilities for understanding ourselves and everything else.

TO PREACH THE TRUTH

If you find it hard to think I'm right about this, I suggest it's only because, when you use the symbol-concept "God," just as when I use it myself, it normally has much more than this purely formal meaning. So far from leaving open the question of just who or what the all-encompassing power really is, our talk about God normally assumes a particular answer to that question, and so also has the material meaning expressed by that answer. Certainly, if we're Christians at all, this is bound to be true of us, because, to be a Christian means, whatever else it means, precisely that all of one's thought and speech about God, and hence about everything else, gives expression to the particular Christian answer to the question of who God really is. But if we ask, then, what it is that determines this Christian answer, there clearly can be only one reply: *Jesus*. So, when we affirm with our lesson that the Jesus who sends the church has himself been sent by God, the question we're ultimately answering is precisely the question of who God is; and our answer to that question, in the words used elsewhere in John's Gospel, is that the only true God is the God who has sent this Jesus (17:3).

The very logic of our lesson, then, forces us to look beyond it to determine who the Jesus to whom it bears witness really is. In fact, this is clearly indicated by the lesson itself. The whole point of Jesus' showing the disciples his hands and his side is to identify himself, now risen and exalted to his Father, as the very one who was crucified.

But if we look at John's Gospel as a whole, there can't be the slightest doubt about the Jesus who was crucified. Put very simply, what John attests throughout his Gospel is that this Jesus is the one through whom each of us has been loved in a decisive way—namely, through his confronting us explicitly with our own possibility of loving. "I give you a new commandment," he says, "that you love one another. Just as I have loved you, you also should love one another. By this, everyone will know that you are my disciples, if you have love for one another" (13:34–35). In other words, precisely in being confronted anew with this commandment, in not being left to ourselves in the bondage of our own lovelessness, but being placed once more under the demand of love, each of us has experienced the gift of Jesus' love that frees us from ourselves to love one another. But, then, to accept this gift of Jesus' love as of decisive significance for our lives is to be able to affirm with our lesson that his love for us, his explicit confrontation with us, is God's own gift to us. Indeed, it is to be able to affirm with the whole of John's Gospel that the love by which we are thus loved by Jesus is nothing other or less than God's own love for the world: not only for you and me and our fellow Christians, but for the world. "For God so loved the world that he gave his only Son, so that everyone who believes in him may not perish but have eternal life. . . . 'And this is eternal life, that they may know you, the only true God, and Jesus Christ whom you have sent'" (3:16; 17:3). "As the Father has loved me, so I have loved you; abide in my love. If you keep my commandments, you will abide in my love, just as I have kept my Father's commandments and abide in his love. . . . This is my commandment, that you love one another as I have loved you" (15: 9–12).

The event we're celebrating today, then, involves nothing less than this: the coming into being of the church as the community of witness to Jesus Christ, and thus as the continuing witness in the world to the gift and demand of love: to the actuality of God's prevenient love for all of us, and hence to our own possibility of returning love for God and for one another. Accordingly, the only good reason for our whole Pentecost celebration is that we ourselves have already been so confronted by this very witness that we can remain the distinctive community we've thereby become only insofar as we not only continue to accept the witness for ourselves through faith, but also continue to bear it for the sake of the whole world in love.

But, this being the case, how we're supposed to celebrate today is no longer in question. We're to celebrate it exactly as proposed by the poet Edmund Spenser in his love sonnet on Easter Day:

Most glorious Lord of life, that on this day
Didst make thy triumph over death and sin;
And, having harrowed hell, didst bring away
Captivity thence captive, us to win:
This joyous day, dear Lord, with joy begin,
And grant that we, for whom thou didst die,
Being with thy dear blood clean washed from sin,
May live forever in felicity.
And that thy love we weighing worthily
May likewise love thee for the same again;
And for thy sake, that all like dear didst buy,
With love may one another entertain;
So let us love, dear love, like as we ought;
Love is the lesson which the Lord us taught.

So let us, too, dear friends, love like as we ought, ever expanding the circle of our love to include any and all of our brothers and sisters. For only by such love, such active concern for the true good of each and every human being, can we properly celebrate the event of the Spirit's coming and of our own coming to be as the church: as the church of the Lord who, teaching such love as a lesson, has thereby given it to us as our own possibility. Nor can the celebration we're presently engaged in here in this service be in any way an exception to this rule. For if what we will have said and sung during this hour has any reason to be at all, it is only that, being our witness to the world that all have the very same possibility of love as we, even it will have been an expression of that same love. Amen.

25 APRIL 1982

Matthew 22:1–14

Once more Jesus spoke to them in parables, saying: "The kingdom of heaven may be compared to a king who gave a wedding banquet for his son. He sent his slaves to call those who had been invited to the wedding banquet, but they would not come. Again he sent other slaves, saying, 'Tell those who have been invited: Look, I have prepared my dinner, my oxen and my fat calves have been slaughtered, and everything is ready; come to the wedding banquet.' But they made light of it and went away, one to his farm, another to his business, while the rest seized his slaves, mistreated them, and killed them. The king was enraged. He sent his troops, destroyed those murderers, and burned their city. Then he said to his slaves, 'The wedding is ready, but those invited were not worthy. Go therefore into the main streets, and invite everyone you find to the wedding banquet.' Those slaves went out into the streets and gathered all whom they found, both good and bad; so the wedding hall was filled with guests.

"But when the king came in to see the guests, he noticed a man there who was not wearing a wedding robe, and he said to him, 'Friend, how did you get in here without a wedding robe?' And he was speechless. Then the king said to the attendants, 'Bind him hand and foot, and throw him into the outer darkness, where there will be weeping and gnashing of teeth.' For many are called, but few are chosen."

There seems to be a consensus among scholars today that, of the two versions of the Parable of the Great Banquet that are preserved in our

99

gospels, it is the Lukan version that is almost certainly the older, not the Matthean one that we've just heard read as our lesson. As a matter of fact, even Luke's version of the parable (Luke 14:16–24) already seems to have undergone a certain amount of development. Unlike Matthew's, it includes two invitations to the uninvited (vv. 22–23), the second of which would appear to be an allusion to the church's mission to the gentiles. But, important as all this may be for the historian of early Christianity, it has no particular importance for us here. It is Matthew's version of the parable that we've heard as our lesson, and our concern must be to come to terms with it.

This we can do only by asking for the word that we're to hear today through the words of the lesson. Obviously, the words themselves are Matthew's, and it's only by reflecting on his words in the larger context of his Gospel that we're likely to grasp their meaning. And yet, as helpful as Matthew's words may be to us, we may be confident that it's not simply them, not simply his particular witness, that either he or the church who preserved and transmitted his Gospel would have us hear. Since the whole purpose of his witness is to reinterpret the original witness of the apostles for his own time and place, and thus to point beyond itself to Jesus Christ, what we must seek to hear in and through his many words is the one word to which they point in its meaning also for us here and now.

I

We may begin by taking a closer look at the text, especially in its differences from the parallel version in Luke' Gospel. Clearly, in both versions, the subject matter of the parable is provided by one of the customs of ancient Palestine that are otherwise familiar to us. When a man in those days wanted to host a banquet, it was customary for him to issue his invitation in two stages: a preliminary announcement to his guests that the banquet would be taking place, and then a final summons to them when all the preparations for it were completed. Just as clear in both versions is the use to which this custom is put in developing the parable. In both cases, the meaning of the parable, as distinct from its subject matter, is evidently the coming kingdom of God, which was typically represented in Jewish tradition as a great feast—as in our Old Testament lesson (Isa 25:6–10a); and the point it wishes to make has to do with the response women and men typically make to the invitation to God's kingdom.

Having received and accepted God's preliminary announcement, those who are invited nevertheless ignore or are indifferent to God's final summons when it calls them to the feast.

But it's just in relation to this meaning or point that Matthew's version of the parable is strikingly different from Luke's. Whereas in the Lukan version, the parable still retains, for the most part, the literary form of a parable, in the Matthean version, it has been almost completely transformed from a parable into an allegory. By "parable" here I mean a relatively simple story whose subject matter serves to make a correspondingly simple moral or religious point, while by "allegory" I understand a relatively more complex story the details of whose subject matter closely parallel and thus illustrate the details of some correspondingly complex moral or religious meaning. Thus, while Luke speaks simply of a man hosting a great banquet, Matthew removes any question as to his meaning by speaking of a king who wills to give a marriage feast for his son and who, as befits a king, is served, not by a couple of slaves but by a large number of them. Still more clearly, the fate of the slaves in Matthew's version is by no means limited simply to encountering the indifference of the invited guests who are now preoccupied with their own affairs. Instead, those "other slaves" whom the king sends with the second final summons are ignored by some of the invited, only to be seized by the rest, mistreated, and then killed. And the king's reaction to all this leaves no doubt as to what Matthew has in mind; for in reporting the rage of the king and his decision to send his troops to avenge his servants by destroying the murderers and burning their city, Matthew alludes unmistakably to the destruction of Jerusalem by the Romans in 70 CE.

Thus, as Matthew gives it, the Parable of the Great Banquet, or of the Wedding Feast, is really an allegory of the history of salvation as seen from the perspective of his own faith and situation as a member of the Christian community. In his view, it is Israel who was originally invited by God, only to refuse God's final summons, both when it was first called by its own prophets and then when it was later called by the apostles of the Christian gospel. And then, because Israel had either ignored or killed the Christian apostles, the coming of Roman troops and their destruction of the holy city is represented as God's act of judgment against a rebellious and murderous people. Indeed, one of the striking things about Matthew's allegory is that it appears entirely to ignore the fact that the first Christians themselves were after all Jews! Whereas Luke seems to allow for an inclusion in the church also of the uninvited within

Israel—"the poor, the crippled, the blind and the lame," as he calls them (Luke 14:21)—Matthew's only invitation to the uninvited is evidently an allegorizing reference to the church's mission to the gentiles. Of course, the main stress even of Luke's version is less to console the uninvited than to pronounce judgment against those who, having been invited, have now refused the final summons—as is clear from the words of the host with which the Lukan version concludes: "For I tell you, none of those who were invited will taste my dinner" (v. 24).

But the greatest difference in Matthew's version is in the ending with which he supplies it. And here we should note three things.

First and most obvious, there's Matthew's addition to the parable, or, rather, his fusion with it, of the other Parable of the Guest without a Wedding Robe. In sharp contrast with Luke, who says nothing of this other parable, Matthew's intention in developing the whole allegory is evidently dependent on the point he intends to make by means of the second parable. What this point is, then, is further indicated by the other two things we need to note: what Matthew expressly implies as to the outcome of the gentile mission; and the generalizing saying he places in Jesus' mouth as the end of the entire passage.

As Matthew has it, "the wedding hall was filled with guests" because the slaves of the king "went out into the streets and gathered all whom they found, both good and bad." The phrase, "both good and bad," is distinctive of Matthew, and it serves to express the view characteristic of his Gospel that the church that has now replaced Israel as God's new people is itself a mixed body containing the unrighteous as well as the righteous. Thus, without doubt, what is pictured in the second Parable of the Guest without a Wedding Robe is that final separation of the good from the bad, which, as we learn from the Parable of the Weeds in chapter 13 (vv. 24–30, 36–43), is not the task of the church, but the task solely of the Son of Man at the last judgment.

Then, finally, there are Jesus' concluding words, "For many are called, but few are chosen" (v. 14). Even though the truth of these words is not literally illustrated by the second parable (according to which, many must be chosen after all, since only one guest is rejected!), there can be little question that Matthew uses the words and the parable together to make one and the same basic point. His main concern, in effect, is to correct the conclusion that those to whom his Gospel is addressed might very well draw from the Parable of the Wedding Feast taken just in itself. For his contemporaries in the church, that first parable might only too easily be taken to mean that, whereas only few were called by God's original invitation to Israel, many have now been chosen by the preaching of the gospel to the gentiles. But Matthew's concern is to deny any such conclusion. Even with the preaching of the Christian gospel, he attests, the distinction remains between the two stages of God's invitation. Although many, indeed, have now been *called* by the gospel, whether any one of them will also be finally *chosen* remains an open question. And the last thought that Matthew wishes to leave with his readers—with each of them singly, as an individual—is undoubtedly to be understood as a warning: "For many are called, but few are chosen."

II

Now what in all this is also intended as a word for us today?

Surely, the first thing we're to hear is the very same word of warning that Matthew addresses to his contemporaries. In one really essential respect—namely, our shared membership in the visible church—our situation today is identical with theirs. We, too, have been invited to God's kingdom by the preaching of the gospel, and we, too, need to be reminded of the nature of that invitation. We, too, need to hear that, in claiming the privileges of the kingdom by entering the church, we must always be willing also to accept its responsibilities—responsibilities that are never exhausted merely by our becoming members of the visible Christian community.

Of course, in hearing this word of warning, some of us today may have more than a little difficulty in appropriating all of the details of Matthew's allegory. In fact, we may feel obliged to say that some of these details tend far more to obscure the word we're intended to hear than to clarify it. By diverting our attention to God's alleged judgment of Israel, the allegory of the king's vengeance against the murderers of his slaves only too easily encourages Christian pride and a false confidence in our membership in the church. But, more than this, who among us can deny that it's just such a representation of the Jews as rebellious and murderous that lies behind the whole tragic history of Christian–Jewish relations—a history that, reaching even into our own century, has led a great council of the Roman Catholic Church to discuss the question whether the Jews are guilty of the death of Jesus Christ: a question even to raise which has been rightly condemned as "fundamentally damaging" to the entire Christian cause?

And yet, important as it is that we be utterly frank about the inadequacy of Matthew's witness at this point, such frankness need in no way interfere with our hearing the word of our lesson also for us. For if we're right in our interpretation of what Matthew is mainly concerned to say, our rejection of these details of his allegory is of no consequence. The word to which he finally points is no wholesale condemnation of Jews, but a retail warning addressed to every single one of us as Christians— this being the very point, we may surmise, of his picturing but one guest who appears at the feast of the king without his wedding robe.

Which raises the question, still unanswered, of just what we're to understand by the missing wedding robe—beyond its somehow representing the unfulfilled responsibilities of God's kingdom, which we never fulfill simply by our membership in the visible church. Just because the parable as Matthew tells it is for the most part an allegory, this has long proved to be a natural, if not an inevitable, question for interpreters to ask in interpreting our lesson. Yet, unless I'm mistaken, we today can hardly accept the answer traditionally given to it. John Wesley, for instance, rightly recognizing that Matthew distinguishes, in effect, between the visible and the invisible church, says of the words, "many are called; few chosen," "many hear; few believe. Yea, many are members of the visible, but few of the invisible, Church." In keeping with this interpretation, then, Wesley identifies the wedding robe as "the righteousness of Christ, first imputed, then implanted." But, as plausible as this answer may have seemed when the unity of scripture could be assumed to be far simpler than it is, we now realize that this answer to our question in terms that Paul might well have used is hardly Matthew's. If we look at what Matthew himself actually says by way of answering it, there can be no mistaking the difference in his answer.

Nor can there be the least question where we should look. For if, as we learned from our study of the lesson, what is pictured in the second parable is precisely the final judgment, with its separation of the bad from the good, there's one passage, above all, that immediately leaps to mind: the great Parable of the Last Judgment in the twenty-fifth chapter of the Gospel, where the king is represented as saying to those at his left hand: "For I was hungry and you gave me no food, I was thirsty and you gave me nothing to drink, I was a stranger and you did not welcome me, naked and you did not give me clothing, sick and in prison and you did not visit me. . . . Truly I tell you, just as you did not do it to one of the least of these [who are members of my family], you did not do it to me" (vv. 42–43, 45). Here, in Matthew's own words, is his identification of the missing wedding robe. What is missing, he tells us, in him who is finally rejected from God's kingdom is not that he has only heard the gospel without believing it, but that he's failed to respond in love to the needs of those around him.

One may urge, to be sure, that none of us is able to respond with such love except with a deep faith in God's love as this is promised to us precisely through the gospel of Jesus Christ. For only when we're freed from undue concern for ourselves by trusting acceptance of God's love for us can we meet the needs of our neighbors as they actually confront us, and for no other reason than that they're there to be met and we're in a position to meet them. But, true as this may be, the fact remains that Matthew's own presentation of the last judgment says not a word about specifically Christian belief. The sole criterion by which the nations are judged is whether they've served the Son of Man by serving their needy neighbors; and if this criterion in any way involves belief, it's only such belief as is necessarily implied by this kind of loving service to those who are in need.

The word Matthew can help us hear, then, is in every sense a radical word. It's the reminder that even the gospel itself, which gathers us into the church, is but the preliminary announcement of God's coming kingdom, the only final summons to which is the summons that comes to each and every one of us, daily and hourly, in the ordinary needs of our neighbors. We're to hear that it is solely in the gift and demand of our neighbors in need that we finally encounter the gift and demand of God. For, although we are indeed called to God's kingdom through the gospel of Jesus Christ, we are chosen for God's kingdom only through our own choosing: only through spending ourselves in love for the sake of a needy world. Amen.

30 May 1982

1 Corinthians 12:1–11

Now concerning spiritual gifts, brothers and sisters, I do not want you to be uninformed. You know that when you were pagans, you were enticed and led astray to idols that could not speak. Therefore I want you to understand that no one speaking by the Spirit of God ever says "Let Jesus be cursed!" and no one can say "Jesus is Lord" except by the Holy Spirit.

Now there are varieties of gifts, but the same Spirit; and there are varieties of services, but the same Lord; and there are varieties of activities, but it is the same God who activates all of them in everyone. To each is given the manifestation of the Spirit for the common good. To one is given through the Spirit the utterance of wisdom, and to another the utterance of knowledge according to the same Spirit, to another faith by the same Spirit, to another gifts of healing by the one Spirit, to another the working of miracles, to another prophecy, to another the ability to distinguish between spirits, to another, various kinds of tongues, to another, the interpretation of tongues. All these are activated by one and the same Spirit, who allots to each one individually just as the Spirit chooses.

Grace to you and peace from God our Father and the Lord Jesus Christ.

This is a special day in the life of our brother who is to be ordained because it publicly marks his acceptance of the church's official call to its representative ministry. But it's also a special day for each of us, because, in the tradition in which we stand, the only essential, or constitutive, ministry of the church is that general ministry to which each of us has been called by her or his baptism and which we've each accepted publicly by becoming a member of the church. Consequently, we cannot play our proper role in the event of our brother's ordination without being mindful of our own. As distinctive as his ministry certainly is, it is but the representative form of the one ministry of reconciliation in which all of us together are given and called to share (2 Cor 5:17–21); and anything that he needs to hear in what will have been said during this hour is something that we, too, should all take to heart—each of us in her or his own way.

Of course, there're varieties of ministry, just as there're many gifts that we together have to discover and develop if we're to accept our own individual calls to it. But there is one gift above all that is necessary to the Christian ministry, especially to the special, representative ministry to which our brother is being ordained; and this is the gift of which Paul speaks in the passage just read for our lesson as "the ability to distinguish between spirits." As a matter of fact, my conviction as a theological educator is that this gift is so necessary to everything that the representative minister is called to do that any theological education that is not specifically devised to develop it cannot possibly achieve its purpose.

Why this is so will become evident if we simply reflect a moment on the situation to which Paul tried to address himself in writing the letter from which our lesson is taken. According to the view now widely held by New Testament scholars, the situation in the church at Corinth with which Paul was concerned was determined above all by a threat to its unity. This threat resulted from the presence within the community of an apparently heterodox, perhaps Gnostic, Christian party. How these heterodox Christians understood themselves can be determined indirectly from the scandals that had arisen in the community, and of which Paul had been informed, as well as from the questions in the minds of his readers to which he evidently tried to respond in his letter. Thus the members of this party appear to have placed a high value on gnosis, or, in our terms, "knowledge" or, possibly, "wisdom"—which is, of course, one reason for suspecting that they may have been Gnostics. And they seem to have thought of themselves as possessing the Spirit, and hence as superior to others in the community, because of such extraordinary manifestations of the Spirit as speaking in tongues. Moreover, because they claimed to possess the Spirit already in the present, they not only denied a future resurrection of the dead, but also regarded themselves as already liberated—enough so, indeed, to have sex with prostitutes and to eat meat sacrificed to idols without the least concern for the scruples of weaker members of the community.

But now, as sharply as Paul had to oppose any such self-understanding in writing to the Corinthian Christians, the fact remained that he and his opponents in Corinth were in extensive verbal agreement. Paul, too, wished to say that Christians possess the Spirit and, therefore, can rightly claim to be liberated as well as to be endowed with special gifts that manifest the Spirit's presence. Consequently, the only tack Paul could take in writing to the Corinthians was the one he in fact did take through his first letter to them—namely, to make certain distinctions: not merely verbal distinctions between different ways of expressing the same Christian self-understanding, but rather real distinctions between radically different understandings of Christian existence, which are not any the less different simply because they're expressed verbally in pretty much the same terms. To make such real distinctions, however, is to exercise just that ability to distinguish between spirits that is spoken of in our lesson; and there's no better commentary on what Paul understood by this gift than he provided by his own example in addressing the situation in the church at Corinth.

I suppose it's unlikely that any of us ever has been or ever will be in just such a church situation—although I've known more than one pastor who allowed as how his congregation could match the one in Corinth any day—scandal for scandal! Even so, I think you must realize just as I do that almost any situation in which we're ever likely to find ourselves as ministers, whether general or special, is going to require us to exercise at least something of this same ability to distinguish between spirits: to make distinctions between what really does manifest the Spirit of God and what is really activated by another and very different spirit, however much it may appear to be one and the same.

Why must we all realize this? Well, the basic reason is that we all know only too well that the most serious threats to Christian existence in our day, exactly as in Paul's, are not those that come from the world outside the church, but those that come from the world inside the church. Although in both cases it's the identical hostile world, whose spirit of self-seeking and boasting is opposed to everything the church stands for, it's all the more dangerous because, being inside the church, it represents itself as of the Spirit of God. Because we all know that we, too, are certain to have to exercise our Christian ministry in face of threats of this kind, we're all aware, at some level, that we must also be able to distinguish between these very different spirits and that Paul's example, accordingly, is immediately relevant also to us.

The peculiar relevance of our lesson, however, as distinct from 1 Corinthians as a whole, lies in what Paul explicitly says about the ability to distinguish between spirits more than in what he himself does in exercising this ability—even, indeed, in this very passage. There are, in fact, three things that we can learn from what Paul has to say here that are of the utmost importance for our own exercise of this ability that is so necessary to our ministry in the church.

The first thing we can learn is that, as necessary and important as the ability to distinguish between spirits certainly is, it is nevertheless not the only spiritual gift but only one gift among many, all given by the same Spirit. "Now there are varieties of gifts," Paul says, "but the same Spirit; and there are varieties of services, but the same Lord; and there are varieties of activities, but it is the same God who activates all of them in everyone." The force of these words in their original context was to counter a claim to superiority, according to which certain gifts uniquely manifest the Spirit's presence and power. As a matter of fact, we probably miss Paul's point if we suppose that the specific spiritual gifts he happens to enumerate make up some kind of an exhaustive list. Far from intending to limit the Spirit's gifts to those he mentions, he's concerned simply to illustrate the several different ways in which that same Spirit becomes present through individual members of the community.

But if any gift of the Spirit is only one among many, it's especially important to remember this in the case of the ability to distinguish between spirits. In the very nature of the case, to reflect sufficiently to make distinctions critically requires that there first be something to reflect on; and so to distinguish between spirits requires that there first be other things going on, or about to go on, with respect to which the distinction between spirits needs to be made—whether these be such extraordinary things as prophecy and healing, the working of miracles and speaking in tongues, or such ordinary things as the church's preaching and teaching and pastoral care. As important as it is that we reflect critically on all of these things, so as to validate the claims to validity that they make or imply—which is to say, so as to distinguish in them between what really is of the Spirit of God and what is really of the other and very different spirit of the world—still, the whole purpose of making this distinction is these other things themselves, so that they may all go on as they ought to do, and claim to do. So the very thing that makes our ability to distinguish between spirits so necessary to everything else we have to do in our ministry also makes it but one gift among others, as dependent on all of them as they all are, in turn, on it.

A second thing we can learn from our lesson about our own attempts to distinguish between spirits is crucial—namely, what the criterion is by which all such distinguishing is to be done. Actually, Paul formulates this criterion in two rather different ways, whose convergence on the same point may not be immediately obvious.

The one way we may call explicitly christological. This is so, at any rate, provided we recognize that the christological assertion, "Jesus is Lord," is properly used to assert not only who Jesus is, but also, and even more fundamentally, who the Lord is, and hence who God is and who the Spirit of God is that is the only Holy Spirit. Clearly, this second use of the assertion is what Paul has in mind when he says that "no one speaking by the Spirit of God ever says 'Let Jesus be cursed!' and no one can say 'Jesus is Lord' except by the Holy Spirit." Paul's way of formulating this criterion, however, is significant. He doesn't say, as Christians have said only too often, that no one can speak by the Holy Spirit except by saying "Jesus is Lord," but only that no one can say, "Jesus is Lord" except by the Holy Spirit. Paul's point, in other words, is in no way to *con*fine the Holy Spirit, but only to *de*fine the Holy Spirit, by making clear that no one speaking in the power of this Spirit could ever say, "Let Jesus be cursed," just as anyone accepting Jesus as Lord can do so only in the power of this same Spirit.

But this christological way of formulating Paul's point remains entirely formal unless and until the Jesus who is Lord is more than simply a name and a title. This is why the other way Paul formulates the criterion is important to the meaning of our lesson. Although he does not explicitly say in this passage just who the Jesus who is Lord really is, he does tell us this implicitly when he explains why, or for what end, the one Spirit, in unity with the one Lord and the one God, gives all spiritual gifts. "To each," he says, "is given the manifestation of the Spirit for the common good." Paul's point, in other words, is that no spiritual gift is given for the merely personal advantage of the one receiving it, as a basis for serving self alone and for claiming superiority over others. On the contrary, every spiritual gift is given for the communal advantage of the entire community, as a basis for serving others as oneself and working together with them for the good of all. But this means that the Spirit of God in whose power one could never say, let Jesus be cursed, and but for whose power one could never accept him as Lord, can only be the Spirit of love. And this implies, in turn, that Jesus himself can only be the very love of God whose Spirit this Spirit is: the very love of God itself made fully explicit as gift and demand through a single human life. Or, in the words of our hymn of response, "Love divine, all loves excelling, joy of heaven to earth come down."

Together, then, Paul's two formulations can teach us the crucial lesson that all our distinguishing between spirits is to be done by reference to Jesus himself as the criterion, which is to say, quite simply, that the real distinctions we have to make are all distinctions between what does and what does not manifest his Spirit, the Spirit of love. For whatever is of the Spirit of God, and not of the spirit of the world, is of the very love that decisively encounters us through Jesus; and this means that, whatever else it may be or do, it in the long run always builds up the church and human community, and never tears them down.

The third and final thing we can learn from our lesson directly follows from the other two. If the ability to distinguish between spirits is one spiritual gift among others; and if the criterion for distinguishing the right use of all such gifts is Jesus himself, or the Spirit of love, then, clearly, our own exercise of this ability is always subject to criticism by exactly this same criterion. In other words, if we've been given the ability to reflect critically so as to distinguish between what is and what is not of the Spirit of God, the end for which we've been given this ability is the very same common good for which all other manifestations of the Spirit are given.

A familiar way of putting this is to say that anyone to whom it is given to speak the truth is always to speak the truth in love. Of course, there's a sentimental way of understanding what love requires that makes it impossible to speak the truth if one loves in this way, because the more one loves, the less one can make the real distinctions between spirits that speaking the truth always requires. But if this understanding of love is not only sentimental, but also deeply wrong, because true love always compels us to speak the truth and to make the distinctions necessary to doing so, still the Spirit of love is not the only spirit that always threatens to manifest itself whenever we exercise our ability to speak the truth and to make such distinctions. As a matter of fact, is there any one of us who has been given this ability, and has then discovered and developed it, who is not continually tempted to misuse it: to manifest through her or his critical reflection, not the Spirit of love, but that other spirit of the world, the spirit of self-seeking and boasting, that always tears down the church and the larger human community the church is called to serve, and never builds them up?

This, of course, is a rhetorical question. But, then, the last thing our lesson can teach us is certainly not the least. All spiritual gifts, Paul concludes, expressly including the ability to distinguish between spirits, "are activated by one and the same Spirit, who allots to each one individually just as the Spirit chooses." Not, please note, as *any of us* chooses, but as *the Spirit of God* chooses—always and only as *the Spirit of love* chooses, and this means always and only for the end of love: never for your or my good alone, but always and only for the common good of all. Amen.

13 JULY 1983

Matthew 5:43–48

"You have heard that it was said, 'You shall love your neighbor and hate your enemy.' But I say to you, Love your enemies and pray for those who persecute you, so that you may be children of your Father in heaven; for he makes his sun rise on the evil and on the good, and sends rain on the righteous and on the unrighteous. For if you love those who love you, what reward do you have? Do not even the tax collectors do the same? And if you greet only your brothers and sisters, what more are you doing than others? Do not even the gentiles do the same? Be perfect, therefore, as your heavenly Father is perfect."

Whitehead makes a comment on Christian theology that repays attention.

> When the Western world accepted Christianity, Caesar conquered; and the received text of Western theology was edited by his lawyers. The code of Justinian and the theology of Justinian are two volumes expressing one movement of the human spirit. The brief Galilean vision of humility flickered throughout the ages, uncertainly. In the official formulation of the religion it has assumed the trivial form of the mere attribution to the Jews that they cherished a misconception about their Messiah. But the deeper idolatry, of the fashioning of God in the image of the Egyptian, Persian, and Roman imperial rulers, was retained. The Church gave unto God the attributes which belonged exclusively to Caesar.

The implications of Whitehead's comment are far-reaching. But its main point is clear enough—and plainly pertinent to much more

113

than merely the work of the theologian. How often we Christians claim to accept Jesus Christ while really ignoring him, while refusing to let our sights be lifted by "the brief Galilean vision of humility." Instead of permitting this vision to revolutionize all our thinking, whether about God or about ourselves, we treat it as something simply to be added to our previous convictions, thereby accepting it only while retaining our deeper idolatries.

Thus we interpret the statement of the Nicene Creed that Jesus is "of one substance with the Father" as though it could mean something else than that the Father is of one substance with Jesus: that the only thing the word "God" can rightly mean for us or for anyone is the "pure un-bounded love" of which Jesus is the sign and seal. And what of our claim that Jesus is "truly man"? Does it signify that we have rethought all that we understand by being human in the light of his humanity? Or does it really mean only that we have used him to sanctify an unreconstructed understanding of ourselves?

So far as the tradition of learned theology is concerned, the answer, I fear, is only too obvious. Exactly as Whitehead suggests, theologians have again and again developed interpretations of human nature and destiny that ignore the revolutionary significance of Jesus Christ. The God of whom they have spoken is not primarily the One whom Jesus re-presents as Father, but the "god of the philosophers," the metaphysical Absolute, whose perfection consists in anything but the perfection of love. And so, too, with their views of man and woman, whom they have more consis-tently interpreted as the "rational animals" of Plato and Aristotle than as the existing selves or persons whom Jesus, together with the prophets of the Old Testament, summons to radical obedience.

But, fateful as it's been, this failure of theology is simply part of a much larger failure in which all of us as Christians have had a part. The vision that Jesus is also flickers uncertainly in churches marked by divi-sions of race and class and in sermons that only too often afflict only the afflicted, reserving their words of comfort for the already comfortable. If the God of Jesus has been misconceived as the indifferent Absolute of the philosophers, God has also been fancied to have a partiality for white skin and male gender and to be a staunch supporter of the United States' national interests. Or, as honesty compels me to add, God's help has only too often been invoked against godless Communism only to put the steel edge of self-righteousness on causes whose justice, when looked at closely, is anything but obvious.

It's hardly surprising, then, that we're often at a loss to understand the words addressed to us in the gospels. Because the convictions we bring to them remain untransformed by the mind of Christ, we either misunderstand them altogether or else find them simply puzzling.

This seems to me especially likely in the case of the familiar saying of Jesus that I have chosen as the text for this homily. "Be perfect, there-fore, as your heavenly Father is perfect." On the usual theological view, it's hard to make any sense of this saying. For, as generally conceived, God's perfection is such that we could never imitate it if we tried, and should never want to imitate it if we could.

God is perfect, we're told, because, unlike us imperfect creatures, God is wholly unrelated to others, and thus exists in complete indepen-dence of the creation. Lest you think I battle straw men, let me cite a few passages from some leading Christian thinkers in our own time.

> The relation between God and his creatures is a wholly one-sided relation, in that while the creation depends absolutely upon God, God in no sense depends upon his creation. God would be neither more nor less perfect if the creation dissolved into utter nothingness. The absolute perfection of perfect being would still exist.

> ♦ ♦ ♦

> God added nothing to himself by the creation of the world, nor would anything be taken away from him by its annihilation— events which would be of capital importance for the created things concerned, but null for Being Who would be in no wise concerned qua being.

> ♦ ♦ ♦

> In view of the widespread tendency even among theologians today to be satisfied with a doctrine of God as in one way or another conditioned by or dependent upon his creation, it is important to stress the absolute necessity of the conception of the entire independence of God. . . . Unless we are prepared to accept the God of classical theism [which is to say, the God who is entirely independent of creation], we may as well be content to do without a God at all.

These theologians also tell us, of course, that God loves his crea-tures. And this might lead anyone who took their statements seriously to suppose that God is somehow concerned with them, and so related to them, after all. But as with one voice, defenders of the theological tradition unite in assuring us that this isn't so. The perfection of God's love, they claim, is that God derives nothing whatever from the being and good of others. His good is something utterly independent of the good of his creatures, and in loving them he himself remains totally unaffected. Thus C. S. Lewis can write: "God is Goodness. He can give good, but cannot need or get it. In that sense, all His love is, as it were, bottomlessly selfless by definition; it has everything to give and nothing to receive."

But if this view of the perfection of God's love were correct, to summon us, as Jesus does, to imitate it would be senseless. The only love we can ever actualize or even conceive can never involve this kind of complete independence. We can love, if at all, not by remaining independent of others, but only by relating ourselves to them; not by being unaffected by their good, but by making their good our very own.

The truth, however, is that it's to just such human love as this that Jesus calls us. And the proof of this is easy: the God whose perfection he attests is not the unrelated Absolute of traditional theology, that idol, who, as Whitehead perceives, is really fashioned in the image of Caesar. No, the God of Jesus is the One whose tender care takes note even of the fall of the sparrow and numbers the very hairs of our head; the One whose own good is not—in Luther's term for sin—*incurvatus in se* (turned in upon itself), indifferent to the weal or woe of others, but a good that consists in nothing except the fullest realization of the good of the whole creation. God is the One who rejoices with all who rejoice and weeps with all who weep, who, as Whitehead puts it elsewhere, is "the great companion—the fellow-sufferer who understands." Or, in the words of William Blake:

> O! he gives to us his joy,
> That our grief he may destroy;
> Till our grief is fled and gone
> He doth sit by us and moan.

Because this is the God to whom Jesus bears witness, his summons to us that we, too, must be perfect is not senseless but full of meaning. It tells us that the true demand that governs our life, even in relation to our enemies, is the love, the sympathetic concern for others, that is embodied from all eternity and to all eternity in God's relation to the world—the God who "makes his sun rise on the evil and on the good, and sends rain on the righteous and on the unrighteous." We humans fall short of real perfection, not because we're related to others and dependent on their good, but because just the opposite is true: because, radically unlike God, who is related to all, we're scarcely related to anyone and can always pursue what we take to be our own good in large measure independently or at the expense of the good of others. To some extent, of course, this imperfection belongs to our very being as creatures who can never be and act as God; even at best, the limits of our sympathy are narrow, and we must always live more or less separated from one another. But we all know, if we're honest, that there's a deeper and more sinister reason for our falling short of God's perfection: we fail to love as God loves, not because we're human, but because we're much less than human—because we do not want even that possible perfection that Jesus demands of us through our lesson.

But his summons to us is not merely a demand; it's also a promise. "Be perfect, therefore, as your heavenly Father is perfect"—that is, not simply *in the same manner* in which God is perfect, which is one meaning of the little word "as," but also *because* God is perfect, which is its other meaning. What finally makes possible even the creaturely and always limited perfection that is the glory of our human life is that each of us, together with the whole creation, is always already embraced by God's pure unbounded love. We are free to love others as ourselves, to find our own good in the good of the whole community of creatures, because, in the words of the First Letter of John, God "first loved us" (4:19). In fact, not even our failure to realize this freedom, our repeated falling short of such love, can ever exclude us from the scope of this promise. Because God is perfect and God's love ever abides as the final fact of our lives, embracing its enemies as surely as its friends, we are continually set free anew to be made perfect in love.

Nor is this true only of those of us who receive this promise decisively through Jesus or through the church that continues his witness by bearing witness to him. The promise of Christian faith is reduced to a travesty if we suppose it to be valid only for the members of a sect that had its beginning some two thousand years ago in Palestine. According to the unambiguous witness of historic Christian faith, Jesus Christ is not merely the founder of yet another religion, but is the expression through one human life of the very Word of God itself: that Word through which, as John's Gospel attests, all things are made and which enlightens everyone (John 1:3, 9). To take this witness seriously is to believe that no person whatever, anywhere, anywhen, exists outside of the ever-renewed promise and demand of God's love. Whether we return this love or not—and we know as Christians that none of us returns it fully and consistently—it is the very atmosphere of our human existence, and no human being could live and breathe for a moment save within its gracious, demanding presence. As soon and as long as we're human at all, or respond ever so faintly or haltingly to the leading of love in our lives, we live only by the prevenient love of God for all of us; and this is true whether we consciously know it or not, and even when we deny with our minds or lips the deep truth that lies ever hidden in our hearts.

All this and more, then, is the meaning of our lesson when we approach it in the light of Jesus Christ. It proclaims the very truth that he himself reveals with utter finality in our human history: that the perfection of life is love and that this perfection is in every moment a new gift and demand to each of us. Amen.

Matthew 28:1–10

After the sabbath, as the first day of the week was dawning, Mary Magdalene and the other Mary went to see the tomb. And suddenly there was a great earthquake; for an angel of the Lord, descending from heaven, came and rolled back the stone and sat on it. His appearance was like lightning, and his clothing white as snow. For fear of him the guards shook and became like dead men. But the angel said to the women, "Do not be afraid; I know that you are looking for Jesus who was crucified. He is not here; for he has been raised, as he said. Come, see the place where he lay. Then go quickly and tell his disciples, 'He has been raised from the dead, and indeed he is going ahead of you to Galilee; there you will see him.' This is my message for you." So they left the tomb quickly with fear and great joy, and ran to tell his disciples. Suddenly Jesus met them and said, "Greetings!" And they came to him, took hold of his feet, and worshipped him. Then Jesus said to them, "Do not be afraid; go and tell my brothers to go to Galilee; there they will see me."

One of the more arresting claims of recent feminist theology is that "Christian faith and community [have their] foundation in the message of the 'new life' proclaimed first by women." The basis for this claim is that, "according to all four gospels, Mary Magdalene is the primary witness for the fundamental data of the early Christian faith: she witnessed the life and death of Jesus, his burial and his resurrection," and "she was sent to the disciples to proclaim the Easter kerygma." Feminist New Testament scholars recognize, to be sure, that even from the beginnings of the gospel traditions there's a tendency to play down the role of Mary Magdalene and the other women as witnesses and proclaimers of the Easter faith. This is certainly the effect of the other main strand of tradition, which Paul cites in 1 Cor 15:3–8, according to which Cephas, or Peter, and the twelve were the principal witnesses, and no mention whatever is made of any of the women. Even so, feminist scholars have a point when they argue for their claim by appealing to one of the usual criteria of exegetical authenticity. That the women were the first witnesses to the resurrection could hardly have been taken over from contemporary Judaism any more than the early Christian church could have invented it. It was not without reason, then, that, long before the modern women's movement, Bernard of Clairvaux spoke of Mary Magdalene and the other women as the "apostles to the apostles." "Christian faith is based upon the witness and proclamation of women."

This is certainly the conclusion one must draw from the Gospel according to Matthew, as is clear from our morning lesson. Mary Magdalene and the other Mary are the first to go to the tomb and to hear the witness of the angel that Jesus has risen. They're also the first to believe this witness and, with fear and great joy, to act on the angel's commission to carry the word of Jesus' resurrection to the disciples. But, most important of all, it is also to the women that the risen Jesus himself first appears—significantly confirming the assurance already given by the angel and repeating the same commission: "Do not be afraid; go and tell my brothers to go to Galilee; there they will see me."

The conclusion is obvious, and to take it to heart is to acknowledge the enormous injustice that has been done and is still being done whenever women in the church are in any way denied the full rights and privileges of their membership just because they're women. But as important as it is for us to recognize this, the deeper meaning of our lesson, if we read it in its larger context, has less to do with vindicating the rights and privileges of the women among us than with underscoring the tasks and responsibilities of all of us, women and men alike.

I've long thought and often said that it's the whole trick of the God of the Bible—in the Old Testament as well as in the New—to turn everything that we would claim merely as a privilege into a responsibility. If Israel is called out by Yahweh, it's only in order to bear witness to God among the nations. And if Paul is made an apostle, it's only so that he can be a minister of Christ Jesus to the gentiles. And so it is also in our lesson: if the women are given to be the first witnesses to Jesus' resurrection, it's so that they can go quickly and tell the disciples that Jesus has risen and is going before them to Galilee, where they, too, will see him.

But, then, of course, what we learn from the conclusion of the Gospel, in the verses immediately following our lesson, is that the same thing happens all over again when Jesus finally appears to the eleven in Galilee: he gives himself to be seen by them on the mountain only in order to issue the same commission to bear witness and to give the same assurance—only more universally: "Go therefore and make disciples of all nations, baptizing them in the name of the Father and of the Son and of the Holy Spirit, and teaching them to obey everything that I have commanded you. And remember, I am with you always, to the end of the age" (vv. 19–20).

We gather this morning at the Lord's table to claim yet again our rights and privileges as children of God and as sisters and brothers of the Lord, and also of one another. Should it be given to us to experience his real presence in the elements of bread and wine, we may be sure that he will commission us, too, to the same tasks and responsibilities to which he called Mary Magdalene and the other Mary: to go quickly and tell all his disciples that he has indeed risen and wills to be seen anew also by them, so that all of us, sisters and brothers together, may carry out his commission to bear witness in and for the whole world. Amen.

22 December 1984

1 Corinthians 13

If I speak in the tongues of mortals and of angels, but do not have love, I am a noisy gong or a clanging symbol. And if I have prophetic powers, and understand all mysteries and all knowledge, and if I have all faith, so as to remove mountains, but do not have love, I am nothing. If I give away all my possessions, and if I hand over my body to be burned, but do not have love, I gain nothing.

Love is patient; love is kind; love is not envious or boastful or arrogant or rude. It does not insist on its own way; it is not irritable or resentful; it does not rejoice in wrongdoing, but rejoices in the truth. It bears all things, believes all things, hopes all things, endures all things.

Love never ends. But as for prophecies, they will come to an end; as for tongues, they will cease; as for knowledge, it will come to an end. For we know only in part, and we prophesy only in part; but when the complete comes, the partial will come to an end. When I was a child, I spoke like a child, I thought like a child, I reasoned like a child; when I became an adult, I put an end to childish ways. For now we see in a mirror, dimly, but then we will see face to face. Now I know only in part; then I will know fully, even as I have been fully known. And now faith, hope, and love abide, these three; and the greatest of these is love.

It's clear from scripture that the difference between man and woman and the companionship between them that this difference makes possible both belong to the good creation of God. In one of the creation stories in Genesis, we read: "So God created humankind in his image, in the image of God he created them; male and female he created them" (1:27). And from the other creation story we learn: "Then the Lord God said, 'It is not good that the man should be alone; I will make him a helper as his partner'" (2:18).

In creating us in God's own image, God also creates us male and female; and God's reason for doing so is quite simply that it's not good for us to be alone. On the contrary, it's good for us to be companions with one another, as well as with God, and so man is to find in woman and—as we may feel bound to stress today—woman is to find in man a fit partner, a suitable companion, for the remarkable venture of human existence.

The name for this unique companionship is "marriage," and this means the human relationship that is based in the erotic love of which we also hear in scripture. In the words of the Song of Solomon, "O that you would kiss me with the kisses of your mouth! For your love is better than wine" (1:2). It is this kind of love that the difference between man and woman makes possible, and it is precisely in it that the whole relationship of marriage has its basis. From a couple's first carefree joys of discovery and courtship to the most tender intimacies of their mature love and the countless responsibilities of founding and raising their family—all this and much more besides is based in that love for one another that God wills in creating them man and woman. Thus we learn from scripture that this kind of love is itself originally and essentially good, so that we are free to participate fully and confidently in all the joys and tasks that are the proper expression of man's love for woman and of woman's love for man.

But the lesson we've just heard teaches us something else. It is not of such love as this that we hear when it speaks of a love that is patient and kind, that is not jealous or boastful, that bears all things, believes all things, hopes all things, endures all things. In fact, in speaking of this very different kind of love, our lesson reminds us that the final good for which each of us is created, the supreme good with which no other can be compared, is a good that is in no way peculiar to the marriage relationship between man and woman. The ultimate good for each of us as persons created in God's image is not the love celebrated in the Song of Solomon—as good as it, in its way, certainly is—but, rather, that other love of which Paul writes so memorably in his letter to the Corinthians. Your end and my end, the final end of us all, is so to know ourselves loved of God through Jesus Christ our Lord that we are freed to love one another in all our human relationships with that other love that is, indeed, patient and kind, as well as all the other things Paul says it is—and more.

What our lesson can teach us, then, is that the unique companionship between man and woman that is marriage is by no means an end in itself. Like every other creaturely good, it, too, is also a means to another end beyond itself: the surpassing end of God's love for all of us and our returning love for God and for all whom God loves.

May God grant that your marriage will be to you just such a means: that its joys and responsibilities may become the "school of charity" in which, growing in grace, you may both increase in the love that never ends even when all else has passed away. Amen.

13 April 1985

Romans 14:7–9

We do not live to ourselves, and we do not die to ourselves. If we live, we live to the Lord, and if we die, we die to the Lord; so then, whether we live or whether we die, we are the Lord's. For to this end Christ died and lived again, so that he might be Lord of both the dead and the living.

My brothers and sisters: grace to you and peace from God our Father and the Lord Jesus Christ.

We gather here this morning to celebrate and give thanks for the life of our dear brother, to come to terms with his death, and to bear witness to our Christian faith: that in life and in death, and in life beyond death, we are not alone; that God is with us, and that God's boundless love encompasses each and every one of our lives even now, when in our sorrow we may not see the way ahead and may not feel the full assurance of God's redeeming presence.

Each of us will remember our brother and give thanks for his life in a different way; and it would become none of us to suppose that he or she could speak for all or even any of the rest of us. Besides, if there is anyone whose life we could not fittingly celebrate with the conventional eulogy for the deceased, it is he. To give thanks for his life to the God to whom he belonged—yes, that he would want us to do. But he would be the first to remind us that God alone is great and that, in the presence of death as at no other time in our lives, we're given to understand why it's solely God to whom all glory is due. Even so, we can no more praise God than serve God in any other way merely abstractly or in general. If it is really to be our praise here and now, we have to offer it concretely and in particular, in terms of our lives as we actually live them with and for one another. For us today, this means that it is in terms of our concrete bonds with our brother and our gratitude for his individual life that we must offer our praise to God.

When I think about my own relation to him, there are three things for which I shall always give thanks.

First of all, there was his loyalty or fidelity, not only to me personally—although that certainly, and in abundance!—but also to the causes to which we were both committed in the context out of which our friendship with one another grew. I refer especially, of course, to the cause of theological education for ministry and for doing theology, which by its very nature involves a whole complex of loyalties: to one's students and to the church that they are called to serve, but also to one's colleagues and to the one task of critical reflection to which all of the theological disciplines and specialties are supposed to contribute. In all of these relations, our brother ever proved himself a loyal and faithful companion, and I think it must have been this that others, also, experienced when they said—as I've heard so many say so often—that he was nothing if not a professional in everything he did. In any event, I have never had a colleague in practical theology whose commitment to the cause of quality theological education was as deeply and consistently supportive of my own.

But hardly less memorable was his robust sense of humor: his infectious sense for the human comedy of which he obviously knew himself deep down to be a part. Rough and ready as it could be sometimes, his was never the standoffish kind of humor that is always bought at someone else's expense, but rather the self-transcending kind that, as Kierkegaard says, is closer to godliness than any other human trait.

Finally, I remember our brother as a man who was profoundly interested in understanding his Christian faith so as to relate it to everything else he understood and to the whole of his life in the world as he actually led it. Of course, he was a theologian, and theologians are commonly supposed to have such an interest as a matter of course. But, as a mutual friend and former colleague of ours used to say, there are two kinds of theologians: the kind who think theologically about theology, and the kind who think theologically about everything. As I knew our brother and shall always remember him, he was emphatically—repeat: emphatically!—the second kind of theologian; and for this, too, I shall ever be grateful.

But, as I said, each of you will have your own memories of his life—even as each of you will also have to come to terms with his death. For myself, I can say only that, as regards the second, I've not been able to think about his death except in relation to Paul's witness in his letter to the Christians in Rome. "We do not live to ourselves," he says, "and we do not die to ourselves. If we live, we live to the Lord, and if we die, we die to the Lord; so then, whether we live or whether we die, we are the Lord's. For to this end Christ died and lived again, so that he might be Lord of both the dead and the living."

In these words, as perhaps nowhere else, Paul points to the underlying ground of our Christian freedom. As Christians, he tells us, we no longer belong to ourselves. We no longer bear the burden of the final care for our lives, for having to secure the ultimate meaning of our existence. No, we've surrendered that burden, yielding ourselves entirely to the grace of God. Therefore, we can enjoy—and I do mean enjoy!—the kind of radical freedom of which Paul speaks elsewhere, when he assures the Corinthians: "For all things are yours, whether . . . the world or life or death, or the present or the future—all belong to you, and you belong to Christ, and Christ belongs to God" (1 Cor 3:21–23).

In other words, our freedom from and for all things is grounded in the fact that "we are the Lord's," and that the Lord to whom we belong himself belongs to God. Paul's point is as simple as it is profound: the only real freedom is grounded in the all-embracing love of God—the love whose gift and demand are made known to us decisively through Jesus. Because the Jesus through whom we encounter this love himself belongs to God, to the mysterious ultimate reality by which all our lives are finally determined, we have been given to understand Jesus as our Lord and this ultimate, all-encompassing mystery itself, as the very love that meets us through Jesus. But, then, insofar as it's no longer ourselves to whom we belong, but Jesus our Lord, our lives are grounded in God's own boundless love and we're set free: free both to live and to die, not any longer to ourselves, but to the Lord, and, through the Lord, to God.

For this reason, Paul tells us, the distinction between life and death—and this means for us here: our life and our brother's death—no longer has the meaning we might otherwise think it to have. Not that there's no difference between life and death, or that we have any reason to be casual about their difference, either in this case or in any other. The point is simply that, as different as they surely are, they're nevertheless both embraced by one and the same love of God and, therefore, by the

Lordship of Jesus Christ, who, as Paul puts it, lived and died to the end that he might be Lord both of the dead and of the living—and this means both our brother's Lord and ours.

In the last words that he and I exchanged—when he first began to suspect that his illness was mortal—it was this point that we found ourselves recalling together. You will understand, then, why I, for one, must think of his death no less than his life as (in the title of one of his books) "proclaiming the word": as a summons to each of us to transcend ourselves into the love of God in Christ Jesus our Lord; to live in the glorious freedom of the children of God; and, therefore, in our own way, ever to seek to understand the faith by which we live, never to lose our sense of humor, and, above all, always to be faithful: always faithful both to one another and to all the causes that unite us in and under the one cause of God's unending love through Jesus Christ our Lord. Amen.

John 10:1–10

"Very truly, I tell you, anyone who does not enter the sheepfold by the gate but climbs in by another way is a thief and a bandit. The one who enters by the gate is the shepherd of the sheep. The gatekeeper opens the gate for him, and the sheep hear his voice. He calls his own sheep by name and leads them out. When he has brought out all his own, he goes ahead of them, and the sheep follow him because they know his voice. They will not follow a stranger, but they will run from him because they do not know the voice of strangers." Jesus used this figure of speech with them, but they did not understand what he was saying to them.

So again Jesus said to them, "Very truly, I tell you, I am the gate for the sheep. All who came before me are thieves and bandits; but the sheep did not listen to them. I am the gate. Whoever enters by me will be saved, and will come in and go out and find pasture. The thief comes only to steal and kill and destroy. I came that they may have life, and have it abundantly."

You'll have recognized by now, I'm sure, that the dominant theme of our lessons this morning is the theme of Christ the shepherd. Of course, we've had the rare treat of hearing the Twenty-Third Psalm, also appointed for today, in the paraphrase of Bach's cantata, "The Lord My Faithful Shepherd Is." But if this has served to highlight the theme in a particularly memorable way, it was also sounded in the reading from the Epistle, in the famous description of Christ as "the shepherd and guardian of [our] souls." Not surprisingly, then, the reading from the Gospel is taken from the very chapter of the Gospel according to John in which the author elaborates the image of Jesus as the good shepherd.

Oddly enough, however, our Gospel lesson doesn't come from the part of this chapter that develops this particular image. The claim that controls it is not, as we might expect, "I am the good shepherd" (vv. 11, 14), but, rather, "I am the gate for the sheep," or, simply, "I am the gate" (vv. 7, 9). Naturally, in the one case as in the other, it's the experience of raising sheep that provides the imagery in terms of which Jesus' claim is made. But there's no getting around the fact, precisely when you take such experience seriously, that there's an important difference between being the shepherd who cares for the sheep and being the gate into the sheepfold through which the shepherd has to pass to get to the sheep or, as the case may be, through which the sheep have to pass if they're to follow the shepherd out into the pasture. Striking about our lesson is that it has been appointed to play this role alongside the other lessons for the day, notwithstanding that it is the image of Christ himself as the gate in terms of which it elaborates its witness.

I have no idea what might explain this, although I certainly regard it as happy, or, if you will, providential. Nothing conduces more to hearing what scripture and the church do and do not have to say to us than recognizing that there are many different ways of making one and the same basic point.

Of course, no one can seriously read the New Testament without in some way recognizing this. If all of its writings bear witness, as they do, to one and the same Jesus Christ, there's no gainsaying that they do so only through many different christologies. The usual way of coming to terms with this is by the thoroughly unhistorical procedure of trying to harmonize the differences. Thus, to take an example that's relevant to this season of the Christian year, no one can deny that the event of the coming of the Holy Spirit, which in the Acts of the Apostles is represented as taking place at Pentecost, fifty days after Easter, is pictured in John's Gospel as having already occurred on Easter evening (Acts 2: 1–11; John 20:19–23). And yet the traditional way of accounting for this difference is to claim that there were actually two comings of the Spirit—the first an earnest, the second its fulfillment—and that both were somehow necessary to the church's constitution as the church.

The advantage of our lesson is that it in no way encourages us to such harmonization. Being the gate of the sheep is different enough from being their shepherd that we're not tempted to say that Jesus must in some way be both. On the contrary, we're encouraged to recognize that the image of him as the shepherd is just that: one particular image, whose basic point can also be made more or less as effectively by means of the other and very different image of him as the gate.

That the two images do, in fact, make the same point may very well explain the choice of our lesson as the Gospel for the day. In any case, there can be no question that the point they make is one and the same.

This is clear enough from the fact that the two claims, "I am the good shepherd" and "I am the gate for the sheep," both have an identical grammatical form, which they share with several other claims that are among the most distinctive things about John's Gospel. I refer to the group of sayings that scholars speak of as "the 'I am' sayings," because they all begin with the same two Greek words usually translated, simply, "I am." In addition to the two we've already noted, they include all of the following familiar sayings:

> "I am the bread of life. Whoever comes to me will never be hungry, and whoever believes in me will never be thirsty." (6:35)

> "I am the light of the world. Whoever follows me will never walk in darkness but will have the light of life." (8:12)

> "I am the resurrection and the life. Those who believe in me, even though they die, will live, and everyone who lives and believes in me will never die." (11:25–26)

> "I am the way, and the truth, and the life. No one comes to the Father except through me." (14:6)

> "I am the true vine." (15:1, 5)

Like the claim, "I am the good shepherd," or "I am the gate," these sayings not only all begin with the identical two-word formula, but are also all obviously symbolic in that they, too, make the claim for Jesus' decisive significance in terms of certain images drawn from ordinary human experience. Thus Jesus can claim to be the way or the true vine in the same sense in which he can claim to be the gate or the good shepherd.

To appreciate the force of any of his claims, however, we need to recognize that the question they answer is not only or primarily the question, Who is Jesus? As they're usually translated, indeed, this is the only question they appear to answer. But one of the peculiarities of Greek is that there is no change in the person of the verb between saying, "I am he" and "It is I," both of these English statements translating the same

Greek phrase. Moreover, careful study of John's Gospel makes clear that the word "I" in the several claims really functions as a predicate rather than as a subject. Consequently, they're properly translated rather differently from the familiar translation. Instead of "I am the bread of life," for example, one would better translate, "The bread of life—it is I." In other words, the question the claim primarily answers is not, Who is Jesus? but Who or what is the bread of life?

If we ask now what kind of question this is, the answer seems clear enough. To ask who or what the bread of life is, or the light of the world, or any of the other things that figure in these sayings, is to ask about who or what one knows oneself to be somehow dependent on if one is to realize one's human existence in a true and authentic way. This assumes, naturally, that, being human, one can never simply live one's life as a plant or an animal can, but must always somehow lead it, and that one can lead it only by understanding it. So, when one asks for the light of the world, say, one asks, in effect, for that understanding of oneself and of the ultimate reality on which one knows oneself to depend that is the true and authentic understanding, as over against all the misunderstandings that leave one to walk only in darkness. Assuming this question, then, Jesus' claim that the light of the world is he asserts symbolically that the understanding of ourselves that we need and ask for simply because we're human is explicitly offered to us decisively through him, in the understanding of our existence to which he calls us.

So, too, with the claim that controls our lesson, "The gate for the sheep—it is I." Here, again, the presupposition of the claim is our question about the true and authentic understanding of ourselves and of the mysterious ultimate reality we have learned to call "God." We ask this question because, like all human beings, we know only too well that it is always possible for us to misunderstand ourselves and God and thereby to miss the abundant life we're always seeking. Indeed, the fact that we find ourselves confronted with contradictory claims on our self-understanding makes us realize that not all who would lead us, and not all the communities we might come to belong to by following them can really be true and authentic. Some of them, by the very logic of the case, are just so many thieves and bandits. And realizing this, we ask for some decisive disclosure of truth and authenticity and can therefore understand Jesus' claim when he asserts symbolically that the gate for which we have been looking is he. For the force of his claim is that the decisive disclosure that we're asking for is the understanding of ourselves that encounters us precisely through him.

Clearly, it is this same basic existential point that is also made, even if in different symbolic terms, by Jesus' other claim to be the good shepherd. In this claim, too, we hear not only or primarily who Jesus is, but also and above all who we are ourselves—namely, those who can find the abundant life for which we yearn only by understanding ourselves and leading our lives as we are given and called to do precisely through Jesus.

But how, exactly, does Jesus give and call us to understand ourselves?

If the claim of our lesson makes the same basic point as any of these other christological claims, it also suffers from the same limitation. In fact, the limitation of all christological claims is that they're purely formal, and insofar empty, if taken simply in themselves. They do serve, indeed, to assert in some terms or other that Jesus is of decisive significance for our lives and for all human lives because what encounters us through him is nothing other or less than the meaning of ultimate reality for us and therewith our authentic possibility for understanding ourselves. But this assertion has no material meaning until we know who Jesus is, in the sense of knowing how we are, in fact, given and called to understand ourselves through him. The limitation of our lesson is that its claim, too, is purely formal as long as we take it by itself, out of its larger context in John's witness to Jesus as a whole.

On the other hand, if we take account of this larger context, there's not the least question about who John represents Jesus to be. He is, quite simply, the explicit act of God's love: the historical fact or event through which the ultimate reality on which we all depend is disclosed to be the unbounded love for us that sets us free to love one another. Thus, according to the best-known passage in John's Gospel, "For God so loved the world that he gave his only Son, so that everyone who believes in him may not perish but may have eternal life" (3:16). Or, again, in the words of the First Letter of John, "God's love was revealed among us in this way: God sent his only Son into the world so that we might live through him. In this is love, not that we loved God, but that he loved us and sent his Son to be the atoning sacrifice for our sins. . . . We love because he first loved us" (1 John 4:9–10, 19).

This witness is also borne by the powerful symbol of Jesus' washing the disciples' feet that John presents in his account of the Last Supper. "Do you know what I have done to you?" Jesus asks. "You call me Teacher and Lord—and you are right, for that is what I am. So if I, your Lord and

Teacher, have washed your feet, you also ought to wash one another's feet. For I have set you an example, that you also should do as I have done to you" (13:12–15). If all this is obviously symbolic, John leaves no doubt about the reality it symbolizes. "I give you a new commandment," Jesus says, "that you love one another. Just as I have loved you, you also should love one another. By this everyone will know that you are my disciples, if you have love for one another" (13:34–35).

Here, my friends, is the reality with which we must come to terms if we're to hear the witness of our lesson—or of anything else that will have been said or sung during this service. However differently it may be expressed, there is only one christological assertion that constitutes all Christian witness—namely, that the ultimate reality with which we each have to do is the reality that is decisively disclosed to us through Jesus. But this assertion remains purely formal, and insofar empty of content, except for the meaning it has solely through Jesus himself: through the fact that we are given and called to believe that the ultimate reality on which we all depend is nothing but love and that we ourselves, therefore, have both the right and the power ever to exist and to act in love.

It is this fact of Jesus, and thus of God's unbounded love for us and of our own possibility of loving one another, that alone gives our lesson its distinctive meaning—that alone allows us to interpret the symbol of the gate or enables us to distinguish the good shepherd from the thieves and robbers, and his own sheep from all the others in the fold. On the other hand, once we come to terms with the fact of Jesus himself, and thus with understanding ourselves as those who are given and called to love decisively through him, there is no mistaking the point of our lesson or of any other christological claim: "Very truly, I tell you, the gate for the sheep—it is I. All who came before me are thieves and bandits; but the sheep did not listen to them. The gate—it is I. Whoever enters by me will be saved, and will come in and go out and find pasture. The thief comes only to steal and kill and destroy. I came that they may have life, and have it abundantly." Amen.

Jeremiah 33:14–16

The days are surely coming, says the LORD, when I will fulfill the promise I made to the house of Israel and the house of Judah. In those days and at that time I will cause a righteous branch to spring up for David; and he shall execute justice and righteousness in the land. In those days Judah will be saved and Jerusalem will live in safety. And this is the name by which it will be called: "The LORD is our righteousness."

There is no question about what the church would say to us by means of our morning lesson. Like the closely parallel verses in an earlier chapter of Jeremiah (23:5–6), and the even more familiar passage in Isaiah that makes use of the same metaphor of a new shoot or branch on an ancient tree (Isa 11:1–5), it prophesies the coming of a new ruler of the house of David. In those days and at that time, it promises, God will cause this new ruler at last to keep God's covenant demand on all of Israel's kings to establish justice in the land, and so fulfill God's promise to his people. Understandably enough, then, Christians have traditionally read our lesson at this season of the church year as a witness to the coming of Jesus Christ. In fact, for countless generations, our mothers and fathers in the church have interpreted it as consciously prophesying Christ's advent as the Son of God who, in the words of one of the earliest Christian confessions, was also descended from David according to the flesh (Rom 1:3).

Of course, for us today this traditional interpretation is quite impossible. As a result of continuing historical-critical study, we now know that our lesson is so far from being a conscious prophecy of the coming of Jesus Christ that some who have studied it the most carefully have seriously questioned whether it is messianic at all, even within the limits of Israel's own hope for the future. Perhaps the most we can say is that it is of a piece with a relatively late projection of Israel's future after the exile, intended to reassure those who had begun to lose hope about the eventual fate of their most cherished institutions: not only the Davidic kingship, but also the Levitical priesthood. At any rate, this clearly seems to be the purpose of the longer passage of which our lesson is a part, with its assurances that God's covenants with his servant David and with the Levitical priests are no less certain to be fulfilled than his covenants with the day and the night, which account for their regular occurrence, each at its appointed time.

But thus to interpret our lesson in its own proper context is to have to face the fact that such reassurance as it offered to those to whom it was originally addressed has long since been proved false by the course of events. With the end of Israel's existence as a nation early in the common era, the institutions of Davidic kingship and Levitical priesthood both ceased to exist, never more to be re-established.

Fully recognizing this, however, we may still see something profoundly right in the church's continuing to use this lesson to bear its Advent witness even today. If its claim is sound that Jesus is the Christ because he is the decisive re-presentation of God's love, then the event of his coming is indeed the fulfillment of all that is true and lasting in every human hope for the future, including the hope expressed in our lesson. Frederick Denison Maurice puts it this way: Being "a revelation of God"

> is not the cold denial and contradiction of all that [women and] men have been dreaming of through the different ages of the world, but rather the sweet reconciliation and exquisite harmony of all past thoughts, anticipations, revelations . . . [T]he Name into which we Europeans have for so many centuries been baptized [is] . . . that which brings all these thoughts at one, separating them from their hateful and degrading additions, raising them to Heaven, and yet establishing a more direct and intimate connection between them and all the daily transactions of this earth.

Realizing this, Christians have never hesitated to appropriate any human hope that they have found either in Israel or among the nations in order to bear witness to Jesus as the one through whose coming all human hopes are at last fulfilled.

But if any hope, in its way, thus anticipates Jesus Christ and, in this rather different sense, is prophetic of his coming, this is uniquely true of the hope of Israel, expressed in our lesson, that, by God's own action, justice and righteousness would someday be established throughout the land. It is precisely this hope for what we today call "social justice" that God has acted decisively to fulfill through Jesus Christ. For although the righteousness that Christ signifies is, in the first place, not our own, but, as Paul teaches us, the righteousness of God, the all-accepting love by which God makes us righteous, still the only way any of us can possibly receive God's righteousness is through a faith that works through love, and this means, through a righteousness of our own for which God's unbounded love sets us free. In this sense, the advent of Jesus Christ is the fulfillment of Israel's hope that God would someday establish social justice. Although a just society can be realized only through our own righteousness, through what we and our fellow human beings do to perform just actions and to establish just structures throughout our social life, with the coming of Jesus Christ God has already done all that God could possibly do toward the realization of such a society by freeing us to realize it.

It is evident to all of us that we as Christians have only too often looked forward to Christ's coming with a narrower hope than the hope expressed in our lesson. In some cases, indeed, we have hoped simply for the fulfillment of our own individual lives, whether in the form of an otherworldly immortality or in the form of an authentic personal existence here and now in this world. In either case, we have narrowed Christ's fulfillment of human hopes down to what only too easily becomes a form of escapism from our responsibility to do justice by working unceasingly for an ever more just society. The abiding importance of our lesson, just as of the Old Testament as a whole, is that it enables us to break out of all such narrowness. It teaches us to widen our human hope so that we hope for nothing less than all that God wills to give us through the coming of Jesus Christ. His coming does indeed re-present the fulfillment of our lives as individuals. But it also re-presents the gift and demand of social justice: of a land that will be saved and a city that will dwell securely, no longer deserving to be called—as in the title of a recent book—"the heartless society," but worthy at last of the name, "The LORD is our righteousness." Amen.

Colossians 3:1–17

So if you have been raised with Christ, seek the things that are above, where Christ is, seated at the right hand of God. Set your minds on things that are above, not on things that are on earth, for you have died, and your life is hidden with Christ in God. When Christ who is your life is revealed, then you also will be revealed with him in glory.

Put to death, therefore, whatever in you is earthly: fornication, impurity, passion, evil desire, and greed (which is idolatry). On account of these the wrath of God is coming on those who are disobedient. These are the ways you also once followed, when you were living that life. But now you must get rid of all such things—anger, wrath, malice, slander, and abusive language from your mouth. Do not lie to one another, seeing that you have stripped off the old self with its practices and have clothed yourselves with the new self, which is being renewed in knowledge according to the image of its creator. In that renewal there is no longer Greek and Jew, circumcised and uncircumcised, barbarian, Scythian, slave and free; but Christ is all in all.

As God's chosen ones, holy and beloved, clothe yourselves with compassion, kindness, humility, meekness, and patience. Bear with one another and, if anyone has a complaint against another, forgive each other; just as the Lord has forgiven you, so you also must forgive. Above all, clothe yourselves with love, which binds everything together in perfect harmony. And let the peace of Christ rule in your hearts, to which indeed you were called in the one body. And be thankful. Let the word of Christ dwell in you richly; teach and admonish one another in all wisdom; and with gratitude in *your hearts sing psalms, hymns, and spiritual songs to God. And whatever you do, in word or deed, do everything in the name of the Lord Jesus, giving thanks to God the Father through him.*

No development in recent New Testament scholarship has been more disturbing to many persons in the church than the findings of a number of scholars concerning Jesus' resurrection. According to one of these scholars, Willi Marxsen, whose conclusion has proved to be particularly controversial:

> We today are no longer in a position to speak of Jesus' resurrection immediately as an event; we must simply say that we have to do with an interpretation, of which persons made use who (at that time!) reflected on their experience. Thus if someone today asks as a historical question, Did Jesus rise from the dead? We can only answer, This cannot be determined. All that can be determined historically (although it can be determined certainly) is that after Jesus' death certain persons claimed to have had an experience that they described as seeing Jesus—and that reflection on this experience led them to the interpretation, Jesus has risen from the dead.

In other words, all that the historian can say about the New Testament witness to Jesus' resurrection is that it is one of the ways, although certainly not the only way, by which the earliest Christian community interpreted its experience of Jesus—more exactly, its experience of Jesus' decisive significance for their own lives as women and men and, as they had come to believe on Easter, for all other human lives as well.

Whatever one thinks of this conclusion, it doesn't take much imagination to understand why so many Christians have been deeply disturbed by it. Given the traditional understanding of Jesus' resurrection not only as a historical event, but also as the event upon which Christian existence is grounded, it is not easy for any of us to allow that talk of the resurrection is really only an interpretation—and only one among other interpretations at that. Easy or not, however, sound historical conclusions cannot continue to be ignored or evaded simply because they overthrow our traditional understandings. This becomes especially clear when, as in the present case, the evidence and arguments that support the conclusion have been marshaled, not by unbelieving historians, but by Christian theologians whose personal commitment to the faith and witness of Easter cannot be seriously questioned.

But even if these theologians are right, and talk of Jesus' resurrection is only one way among others of interpreting his decisive significance, no one questions the centrality of this interpretation for most of the New Testament witnesses. Nor does anyone wish to question that more than one of these early witnesses so develops this way of interpreting Jesus' significance as to interpret our own existence as Christians as our sharing in his resurrection, as our having been raised with Christ. Among these witnesses is the author of the Letter to the Colossians, and the passage from this letter that has been read as our morning lesson is a particularly striking example of just such an interpretation.

Clearly, the idea that Christ has risen from the dead and that we as Christians have been raised with him is the controlling idea throughout this passage. "So if you have been raised with Christ," it asserts, "seek the things that are above, where Christ is, seated at the right hand of God. Set your minds on things that are above, not on things that are on earth, for you have died, and your life is hidden with Christ in God. When Christ who is your life is revealed, then you also will be revealed with him in glory." But if the idea of Christians having been raised with Christ clearly controls the forms of expression in our lesson, there can be no question about the basic point that it thereby seeks to make. Certainly, if we take account of its larger context in the Letter to the Colossians as a whole, we can say with confidence that its basic point, as distinct from its forms of expression, is precisely the meaning of Christian existence, given the decisive significance of Jesus Christ.

It is this same question, then, about what it means to exist as Christians with which we must approach our lesson if we would hear what it has to say to us today—keeping in mind that its answer to this question is naturally cast in its terms rather than in ours and that we cannot reasonably expect to hear its answer except by recasting it in terms that are our own.

What does it mean, then, for us to exist as Christians if, as our lesson puts it, we have been raised with Christ?

It means, first of all, that *the new existence that is ours as Christians is not something for which we have yet to wait in the future, but something in which we already find ourselves here and now in the present.* This first point in our lesson's answer to our question is not so much asserted as assumed. This is clear from the way it begins: "So if you have been raised with Christ, . . ."—a formulation that evidently presupposes that the Colossians have already been raised with Christ. Indeed, it's only because our lesson presupposes this that it can proceed to summon the Colossians to "seek the things that are above." The imperative it asserts rests on the indicative it begins by presupposing. Nor is there any question about its reason for presupposing this indicative if we recall what has already been said earlier in the letter. The assertion that the Colossians have died and been raised with Christ clearly refers back to a statement in the preceding chapter: "when you were buried with [Christ] in baptism, you were also raised with him through faith in the power of God, who raised him from the dead." Thus "when you were dead in trespasses and the uncircumcision of your flesh, God made you alive together with him, when he forgave us all our trespasses, erasing the record that stood against us with its legal demands. He set this aside, nailing it to the cross" (2:12–14).

A similar reference to Christ's work of reconciliation, as well as, it would seem, a clear allusion to baptism, also occurs in chapter 1, when the author asserts that God the Father "has rescued us from the power of darkness and transferred us into the kingdom of his beloved Son, in whom we have redemption, the forgiveness of sins" (1:13–14). Here, again, the essential point is that this deliverance or transfer has already happened. Through the event of Jesus Christ, and through the baptism whereby we have each been given to share in this event, we have already been placed under the rule of God's love, and, through our own obedient faith in that love, we are already delivered from both the guilt and the power of sin. In this sense, our being raised with Christ, and thus our new existence as Christians, does not lie ahead of us in the future but is already a present reality.

This is not to say, however, that our lesson in no way points us to the future. On the contrary, it is express in affirming that the new life that is already ours through baptism and faith is still hidden and will not become apparent until Christ himself finally appears. "You have died, and your life is hidden with Christ in God. When Christ who is your life is revealed, then you also will be revealed with him in glory." What is still to come, to be sure, is not our resurrection with Christ; for that, as we have learned, is already real in the present through the grace of our baptism and our own faith in God's love. Nevertheless, because the only ultimate ground of our existence is precisely God's love as it is made known to us through Christ, the new life that is already ours is nothing other than our life in God's love and, in this sense, it does indeed always lie ahead of us in God's unending future.

And this explains why our lesson makes a second point in response to our question about the meaning of Christian existence—namely, that *the new existence that is already ours is not something that we ever simply are, but something that we must ever again become.* Because our new life is not our own, but is hidden with Christ in God's love, we can lay hold of it only through faith and hope—and this means, only through believing and hoping ever again anew in each and every moment of our lives.

This is clearly what our lesson teaches us when, having assumed that the Colossians have already been raised with Christ, it nevertheless goes on to exhort them, "seek the things that are above," "set your mind on things that are above, not on things that are on earth." By "the things that are above" here is evidently meant what the author earlier speaks of as "the hope laid up for you in heaven," of which the Colossians have already heard in "the word of the truth, the gospel" (1:5). But this hope is clearly an objective rather than a subjective hope; it is the hope *for which* believers hope, rather than the hope *through which* they hope. Thus, having assured the Colossians that Christ has reconciled them by his death, in order to present them holy and blameless and irreproachable before God, the author can only add, "provided that you continue securely established and steadfast in the faith, without shifting from the hope promised by the gospel that you heard" (1:22–23).

So it is that the dominant mood of our lesson is not indicative but imperative. Although it begins by presupposing that we already are who we really are, it itself consists in one summons after another to become who we really are. "Seek the things that are above. . . . Set your minds on things that are above. . . . Put to death whatever is earthly in you, . . . seeing that you have stripped off the old self with its practices and have clothed yourselves with the new self, which is being renewed in knowledge according to the image of its creator. . . . And let the peace of Christ rule in your hearts, to which indeed you were called in the one body. And be thankful. Let the word of Christ dwell in you richly; teach and admonish one another in all wisdom. . . . And whatever you do, in word or deed, do everything in the name of the Lord Jesus, giving thanks to God the Father through him."

But if our lesson thus teaches us that we can exist in this new way, and so be who we really are, only by ever and again becoming who we really are, there is yet a third point we can learn from it about our existence as Christians. It also teaches us that *the new existence that is already ours is not something that in any way removes us from our ordinary relationships to one another, but something that in every way transforms us in these very relationships.* The most striking thing about our lesson is that its metaphysical contrast between "things that are above" and "things that are on earth" is at one and the same time the moral or ethical contrast between two radically different ways of acting toward others. Thus its summons, "set your minds on things that are above, not on things that are on earth," is unpacked by the summons, "Put to death whatever in you is earthly: fornication, impurity, passion, evil desire, and greed (which is idolatry) . . . you must get rid of all such things: anger, wrath, malice, slander, and abusive language from your mouth. Do not lie to one another, seeing that you have stripped off the old self with its practices and have clothed yourselves with the new self, which is being renewed in knowledge according to the image of its creator." In positive terms, then, this becomes the further summons, "Clothe yourselves with compassion, kindness, humility, meekness, and patience. Bear with one another and, if anyone has a complaint against another, forgive each other; just as the Lord has forgiven you, so you also must forgive."

Thus the last point our lesson makes in response to our question is that our new existence in faith and hope is also an existence in love. "Above all," it tells us—or, as John Calvin thinks we should translate, "for the sake of all"—"clothe yourselves with love, which binds everything together in perfect harmony." Just as the Christ with whom we have been raised is none other than the Jesus through whom we have been explicitly called to faith and hope in God's love, so to be raised with this Christ is nothing other than to exist in the love to which Jesus calls us: in returning love for God and, in God, for all whom God also already loves.

Nor is our lesson entirely without indication of the specifically political implications of this existence in love. Here, it says, "there is no longer Greek and Jew, circumcised and uncircumcised, barbarian, Scythian, slave and free; but Christ is all and in all." Just as the lordship of the risen Christ relativizes all the divisions between human beings erected by society and culture, so within the dominion of his lordship none of these divisions can set limits to the scope of the love in which we are called to exist. Although our life together continues to be marked by real social and cultural differences, they no longer count as reasons, or excuses, for not loving beyond them. On the contrary, our being called to love beyond and in spite of all such differences also provides the best of reasons for transforming any social and cultural structures by which the differences between human beings become hardened into divisions. And this is true even if we owe the full sense of the political meaning of love not only to the demand of love itself, but also to our distinctively modern consciousness of responsibility for the whole of our common life. For us today, certainly, the love to which our lesson calls us can and must become incarnate not only in just actions toward individual persons within society and culture, but also in an unceasing quest for ever more just structures of society and culture themselves.

Is talk of Jesus' resurrection really only an interpretation, then? Well, even if it is nothing more than an interpretation, we now know what it's an interpretation of and that what it interprets is, or at least can be, a very real event in the life of each of us—insofar, namely, as through obedient faith in God's boundless love for us through Christ we are so freed from ourselves as ever to hope and to love, and, therefore, to seek justice for all who are wronged and oppressed by things as they are.

Grant, O God, that we who have been raised with Christ in baptism may ever continue in the faith, stable and steadfast, not shifting from the hope of the gospel, and abounding in love for one another and for all whom you give us to love and to serve; through the same Jesus Christ our Lord, who is seated at your right hand. Amen.

Romans 12:1–8

I appeal to you therefore, brothers and sisters, by the mercies of God, to present your bodies as a living sacrifice, holy and acceptable to God, which is your spiritual worship. Do not be conformed to this world, but be transformed by the renewing of your minds, so that you may discern what is the will of God—what is good and acceptable and perfect.

For by the grace given to me I say to everyone among you not to think of yourself more highly than you ought to think, but to think with sober judgment, each according to the measure of faith that God has assigned. For as in one body we have many members, and not all the members have the same function, so we, who are many, are one body in Christ, and individually we are members one of another. We have gifts that differ according to the grace given to us: prophecy, in proportion to faith; ministry, in ministering; the teacher, in teaching; the exhorter, in exhortation; the giver, in generosity; the leader in diligence; the compassionate, in cheerfulness.

My brothers and sisters in Christ, we gather this evening as a Christian community to celebrate yet again the service of word and table. Of course, the occasion for our gathering is special, in that some among us, having now finished their course of study in the School of Theology, are to be awarded their degrees tomorrow at the commencement convocation of the University. Beyond any question, this is a special moment in their lives, marking at once the ending of a time of preparation and the beginning of the time of service for which they have been preparing. But for all the rest of us, also—families and friends, fellow students and teachers, administrators and staff—it is a special event, having no exact precedent and never to be repeated. Each graduating class, no less than each graduating student is unique; and so this service of worship, as much as it is like what Christians have gathered to do from the very beginning of their community, is a unique moment in the lives of each and every one of us.

And there is another respect in which it is different, if not unique, in comparison with other services with which we're all familiar. Although we're gathered as one Christian community around one word and one table, we're also unusually many, the diversity we represent being hardly less striking than our unity. In addition to all the usual differences found in Christian communities—of gender and race, ethnic background and class, as well as between clergy and laity—our community here not only includes differences between church and academy and students and faculty, but also embraces the variety of special ministries and all the different programs of study developed to prepare for them. It is also a remarkably international community, including persons from just about every continent and representing quite diverse nationalities, languages, and cultures. So as certain as it is that we are one, we're just as certainly many; and a keen sense that this is so can hardly escape us as we gather for this service of Christian worship.

Insofar as we are struck by this, however, we ought to be open to hear what God would say to us through the words of Paul to the Christians in Rome, which have been read as the lesson from the Epistle. For Paul's concern in these words is to say as simply and straightforwardly as possible what we Christians all need to hear in every moment of our lives—most especially in moments such as this, when, faced with a new and different future, we may be struck at once by our unity and by our difference as a community and may thus be led to ask about them in a new way.

Paul takes for granted that our unity and difference as Christians are equally real and important and that neither, therefore, should ever be ignored or played off against the other. Through Christ, God calls all of us to the same Christian existence in and for the world; and yet an essential part of this one Christian existence is that each of us is called to it in her or his own way—not so as to exclude our differences as individuals, but so as to include them, as themselves gifts of God's grace, all of which are to be used in some way to build up the one community for its mission to the world. But just because our oneness as Christians is not simply other than our differences but itself includes them, Paul naturally begins with it, addressing his readers precisely in their unity. "I appeal to you therefore, brothers and sisters, by the mercies of God, to present your bodies as a living sacrifice, holy and acceptable to God, which is your spiritual worship."

Paul's language here repays attention. His question, obviously, is as to the nature of the service or worship of God that all of us as Christians are bound to offer. And he first speaks of this in the language of cult or formal worship and, specifically, of cultic sacrifice, although with the significant difference that the sacrifice he calls Christians to offer is not the dead sacrifice of some animal but a living sacrifice of themselves. But no sooner has he spoken in these terms than he shifts to the very different language of one of the philosophies of his day, which typically contrasted the bloody sacrifices of popular religion with the intellectual devotions or meditation proper to philosophy by calling the second "our spiritual (or reasonable) worship." Paul's point, then, is that Christian worship, in its deeper meaning, is something other and more than cult, or formal worship—not only of the kind involving blood sacrifices, but even of the relatively more "spiritualized" kind of which our service of worship here is an example. Important as any such service may be in representing our deeper worship and providing means for celebrating it explicitly, our worship itself is something other and more profound than all religion. On the other hand, it's not philosophy, either, because it's the offering to God, not just of our minds, but, as Paul puts it, of our "*bodies*," by which he means our whole beings as selves, who exist only in relation to the world of others whom God gives us to love and to serve. Yes, this is our spiritual worship: so to entrust ourselves to the mercies of God for each of us as to be freed to give ourselves wholly to God: loving and serving God by all that we think, say, and do precisely by loving and serving all whom God loves.

Having made this clear, Paul once again abruptly shifts language— this time by employing the contrast commonly drawn in the early church between this world, or this age, and the coming world, or age, of God's rule. To Paul's mind, as to the minds of early Christians generally, God's new world had already drawn near and become really present through the event of Jesus Christ. Therefore, to understand oneself anew as one is given and called to do through this event was to live, even in the midst of this world, as one who already belongs to the world to come ruled by God's love. With this in mind, Paul can make the same point about our oneness as Christians in a significantly different way: "Do not be

147

conformed to this world," he says, "but be transformed by the renewing of your minds, so that you may discern what is the will of God—what is good and acceptable and perfect."

The key question here is just what it means to be conformed to this world. It clearly seems to mean not only doing the things that this world does, but also doing them in the way, or after the manner, in which the world does them. But, more fundamental still, it means existing in this world for this world's reasons—so as thereby to secure the meaning of our lives ourselves, by what we ourselves are or have or do, instead of simply accepting the security of God's utterly free and unbounded love. Not to be conformed to this world, then, is to abandon all of our characteristically human attempts at self-contrived security and to entrust ourselves completely to the mercies of God. And so Paul can also speak of this transformation positively by appealing for the renewing of our minds, in the sense of this new self-understanding, this new understanding of ourselves as always already secure in God's love. With this, he says, we no longer need to be blind to God's will for our lives, but may rather discern God's will precisely by knowing what is good and acceptable and perfect.

But having thus appealed to us in our oneness as Christians, Paul immediately turns to the individual differences that our oneness itself includes. On the authority of his own difference in the grace given to him as an apostle, he says to each of his readers individually, "Do not think of yourselves more highly than you ought to think, but think with sober judgment, each according to the measure of faith that God has assigned." This is evidently the same appeal that he has just made to all of his readers collectively, only now formulated to take account of each of them as an individual in her or his differences from others. If to be conformed to this world, finally, is to exist for this world's reasons, so as to secure the meaning of our lives ourselves instead of simply trusting in the security of God's love, it is also to think of ourselves more highly than we ought to think.

Yet we need to be careful here lest we miss what Paul wants to say. It lies in the nature of the case that if we suppose we can secure the meaning of our lives ourselves, by what we are or have or do, we greatly overestimate our powers as mere creatures who ever remain absolutely dependent upon God for our being and meaning. But this naturally leads those of us who are relatively powerful and advantaged by things as they are to overvalue our differences in comparison with those of others, whom we think of more lowly than we ought to think, thereby tempting them, also, not to overvalue, but to undervalue their individual differences. The result is that the great temptation of all who are relatively powerless and disadvantaged by things as they are—whether because of gender, race, class, or culture—is not to think of themselves more highly than they should but less. Consequently, as feminist theologians in particular have helped us see, to heed Paul's appeal to think of ourselves as we ought to think, with sober judgment, each according to the measure of faith that God has assigned us, is to avoid undervaluing our differences just as much as overvaluing them. "For as in one body we have many members, and not all members have the same function, so we, who are many, are one body in Christ, and individually we are members one of another."

But to relate to one another in this way is neither to overvalue our individual differences nor to undervalue them, but to look upon all of them alike—those of others equally with our own—as gifts of God's grace, all given for building and strengthening the one body in Christ for its mission to a needy world. "We have gifts that differ," Paul says, "according to the grace given to us: prophecy, in proportion to faith; ministry, in ministering; the teacher, in teaching; the exhorter, in exhortation; the giver, in generosity; the leader, in diligence; the compassionate, in cheerfulness." Paul hasn't the least intention, obviously, of giving anything like an exhaustive list of our different individual gifts. He simply mentions some that he judges central to the mission of the church. And his point in doing so is just as obvious: he wants each of us as Christians to use our different gifts, whatever they may be, in accordance with their own inherent purpose, neither overvaluing them nor undervaluing them, whether they be our own or those of other members of the one body. Each gift is given for the sake of the whole church, which itself exists, in turn, for the sake of the whole world: to bear witness to all of the mercies of God, and so itself, as church, to be one of these mercies.

I appeal to you, therefore, brothers and sisters, by the mercies of God, to present your bodies as a living sacrifice, holy and acceptable to God, which is your spiritual worship. Do not be conformed to this world, and so do not think of yourself either more highly or more lowly than you ought to think. But being transformed by the renewing of your minds, so that you may discern the will of God, think of yourself with sober judgment, each according to the measure of faith that God has assigned you. For as in one body we have many members, and not all members have the same function, so we, who are many, are one body in Christ if we relate to one another as its individual members. Having, then, gifts that differ according to the grace given to us, let us use them as members of the one body, so as not just to know God's will, but to do it—to do what is good and acceptable and perfect. Amen.

6 July 2003

Romans 6:3–11

Do you not know that all of us who have been baptized into Christ
Jesus were baptized into his death? Therefore we have been buried
with him by baptism into death, so that, just as Christ was raised
from the dead by the glory of the Father, so we too might walk in
newness of life.

   For if we have been united with him in a death like his, we will
certainly be united with him in a resurrection like his. We know
that our old self was crucified with him so that the body of sin might
be destroyed, and we might no longer be enslaved to sin. For who-
ever has died is freed from sin. But if we have died with Christ,
we believe that we will also live with him. We know that Christ,
being raised from the dead, will never die again; death no longer
has dominion over him. The death he died, he died to sin, once for
all, but the life he lives, he lives to God. So you also must consider
yourselves dead to sin and alive to God in Christ Jesus.

Nothing is more obvious, if we stop to think about it, than that we can
live out our Christian existence only in our own time and place in history
and in its forms of life and thought. But, as obvious as this may be in
our own case, it's likely to be anything but obvious when we turn to the
Christian existence documented by the writings of the New Testament.
Just because these writings go to make up *the Bible*, which we acknowledge as in some way God's word to us, and insofar the rule and guide of
our own lives as Christians, we tend to forget that the forms of life and
thought that we find in them are those of an earlier time and place, not
at all different in this respect from our own. And yet, if the words of the

151

Bible are ever really to become God's word to us, we must learn to read and hear them, first of all, as the words of human beings: human beings like ourselves, through whom the word we are to hear as God's word is always expressed only more or less adequately and fittingly. And this is certainly true of Paul's words in his letter to the Romans that we've just heard read as our Epistle lesson this morning.

"Do you not know," Paul asks, "that all of us who have been baptized into Christ Jesus were baptized into his death?" The very way he asks this indicates that he counts on his readers being well aware of what he would remind them of. And what is that? Well, it's the fact that baptism is the initiation sacrament of the Christian community, which as such imparts to each individual initiate participation in the death and resurrection of Jesus Christ. How so?

The short answer is: in much the same way in which certain other religions, widespread in Paul's time and place, understood their initiation sacraments to impart a share in the destiny of their particular deities. You see, even the early Christian communities before and during Paul's time were in essentially the same situation in which we find ourselves today. No more than we did they create the concepts and terms in which they naturally thought and spoke; rather, they inherited these, or borrowed them, exactly as we do, and, very much like us, they could communicate successfully with others only in common forms of thought and speech. Consequently, in order to think and speak about the meaning of Jesus Christ in a way that not only they themselves, but also persons outside their communities could understand and, as they hoped, make their own, they naturally took over concepts and terms that were already in circulation and more or less widely shared.

Among the more influential of these, as it turned out, were the forms characteristic of the so-called mystery religions. To go into any detail about these religions would require giving just that long answer to our question that is neither possible nor necessary here. Suffice it to say, simply, that, by the time Christianity emerged, certain religions that had originated as vegetation cults in the ancient Near East had gradually made their way into the larger Greek-speaking world—the "ecumene," as it was called—where they enjoyed an extended, even if transformed, lease on life. Especially to the masses of the larger urban areas, their typical teaching concerning the destiny of a young god who suffered death only to be reawakened to life spoke to a deeply felt need. Anxious about the transience and death of which their lives in this world had made them acutely conscious, they responded enthusiastically to the message that, by being baptized into the death of such a god, they, too, could die to death and look forward to a blessed immortality.

Now these forms of thought and speech typical of the mystery religions provide the language for our lesson. On the understanding Paul assumes in his readers, baptism brings it about that the destiny of the cult deity, Christ Jesus the Lord, avails for initiates into the Christian mystery just as if it were their own destiny. By being baptized into his death, they are given to share also in his resurrection.

So far, then, we have Paul the man of his own time and place, thinking and writing in its forms of thought and speech—in this case, the forms typical of the mystery religions. But the striking thing about our lesson is the distinctive spin that Paul then gives to this understanding of baptism and of the decisive significance of Christ's death and resurrection.

According to the mysteries, the purpose of the baptism constituting their initiation sacrament was to assure the initiate of her or his participation in immortality: in a future life beyond our life in this world and in spite of the death that ends it. And so, on this understanding, one would naturally expect Paul to proceed by saying, "Therefore we have been buried with him by baptism into death, so that, just as Christ was raised from the dead by the glory of the Father, we, too, might be raised from the dead." But, of course, this is not what Paul says. The purpose of our baptism as Christians, he tells us, is distinctively different: it is "so that we might walk in newness of life." What our Christian initiation sacrament represents to us is not only, or even primarily, assurance of a future life beyond death, but rather a new possibility for living our lives here and now in the present, in our relations with one another, and in meeting the obligations that these relations lay upon us.

That this is so is fully confirmed by how Paul uses the same language elsewhere. So far as the verb "to walk" is concerned, he follows Hebrew usage and consistently means by it such things as to live in a particular manner; to lead one's life in a certain way; to follow a certain course; to behave in this way rather than that; to conduct one's life or oneself in a certain way; or—as we might be inclined to translate today—to follow a certain life-style. So he says to the Galatians, "If we live by the Spirit, let us also walk by the Spirit" (Gal 5:25). And in the same vein, he can talk positively about walking "according to the Spirit" (Rom 8:4), living "honorably as in the day" (Rom 13:13), "worthy of God, who calls you into his own kingdom and glory" (1 Thess 2:12), and "walking in love"

(Rom 14:15), just as he can talk negatively about walking "according to the flesh" (Rom 8:4), "according to human inclination" (1 Cor 3:3), "in reveling and drunkenness, in debauchery and licentiousness, in quarrelling and jealously" (Rom 13:13), and "no longer walking in love" (Rom 14:15). As for the rest of the phrase, it, too, involves a Hebraism by speaking with the substantive of "newness of life," instead of using the adjective to say, simply, "new life." But, again, its reference, unmistakably, is not to any future life after death but to our present life here and now, and it means a way of living this life that is unusual, unheard of, marvelous, indeed, eschatological—as it clearly is when Paul speaks elsewhere of a "new creation," as, for example, in 2 Corinthians 5:17, when he says, "If any one is in Christ, there is a new creation: everything old has passed away; see, everything has become new!" or in Galatians 6:15, when he says, "For neither circumcision nor uncircumcision is anything but a new creation is everything!"

Of course, Paul doesn't question for a moment that Christ's death and resurrection and, therefore, our own baptism, also represent to us a future victory of life over death. In fact, he goes on to affirm that "if we have been united with [Christ] in a death like his, we will certainly be united with him in a resurrection like his." Even so, the eminently this-worldly thought that dominates Paul's mind is very different from the exclusively otherworldly conception of the typical mystery religion. "We know that our old self was crucified with [Christ in baptism] so that the body of sin might be destroyed, and we might no longer be enslaved to sin. For whoever has died is freed from sin." The death that Christ died "he died to sin, once for all," and the whole point of his death, and hence also of our baptism, is to free us from sin, so that with him, we, too, might live to God. Thus the lesson concludes, "So you also must consider yourselves dead to sin and alive to God in Christ Jesus."

But please note the grammar of this formulation: it's not in the indicative mood, but in the imperative. It doesn't just assert what we are but rather summons us to understand ourselves in a certain way—namely, as persons who are already dead to sin and alive to God in Christ Jesus. And the reason Paul puts it this way is clear, being immediately implied by his understanding of the meaning of Christ and of our baptism as Christians. Because the newness of life to which we are freed in Christ is precisely a matter of "walking," of how we understand ourselves and lead our own individual lives here and now in this world, what our baptism represents to us is really only a new possibility: a possibility that we ourselves must each actualize again and again anew, in every new situation, by our own free and responsible decisions. To be sure, we *are* dead to sin, but this is only because, or insofar as, we ever and again *become* dead to sin by understanding ourselves anew to be exactly that. Although God's loving acceptance of us has been revealed once for all through Christ Jesus, as re-presented to each of us individually through the once-for-all sacrament of our own baptism, it's only through our own ever renewed acceptance of God's acceptance through faith, and in our actual walking, in the actual leading of our lives, that it is the newness of life to which God would call us through our lesson.

Nor is there any question about the connection of this call with the other sacrament that we're specially gathered here this morning to celebrate. For Paul himself says of the Lord's Supper, "as often as you eat this bread and drink the cup, you proclaim the Lord's death until he comes" (1 Cor 11:26). In other words, the sacrament we're about to celebrate but confirms to us yet again the same gift and demand that are re-presented to us through our baptism as well as through the words of our lesson. It re-presents to us that same possibility of leading our lives through faith in God's love for us and in returning love both for God and for all whom God loves.

Of course, it's not only or even primarily here, in the gathered church, that we're given and called so to lead our lives. In fact, we in no way miss Paul's meaning if we apply to baptism and the Lord's Supper, as well as all the rest of our religious life as Christians, what he himself says concerning circumcision. There are three passages in particular from whose close parallelism we can learn as much, I believe, as from any other three passages in scripture. I cited one of them a moment ago: "For neither circumcision nor uncircumcision is anything but a new creation is everything!" (Gal 6:15). But hear now the other two: "Circumcision is nothing, and uncircumcision is nothing; but obeying the commandments of God is everything" (1 Cor 7:19). And "in Christ Jesus neither circumcision nor uncircumcision counts for anything; the only thing that counts is faith working through love" (Gal 5:6).

What, then, is the "new creation," or the "newness of life," of which Paul speaks? Well, here you have his answer in his own words: it is "obeying the commandments of God," or—since he teaches that all of God's commandments are summed up in the one word, "Love your neighbor as yourself" (Rom 13:9)—it is "faith working through love."

Paul's point, in a word, is that nothing specifically religious, any more than its contrary—be it baptism, the Lord's Supper, or anything else we do as a gathered community, or that other human communities outside of ours omit to do—none of this is finally of any avail, but only a new creation, only obeying the commandments of God, only faith working through love. And the proving ground of such a faith is always the same: the one needy world in which we each live here and now. And the only way we can prove it is by identifying with this world in its always tortuous and ambiguous struggles to become more human, to achieve forms of life and structures of thought, action, and social organization through which the good of life that God intends for all creatures can be more fully realized and generously shared.

Still and all, the irreplaceable significance of the Lord's Supper and our baptism as well as all the rest of our religious life, is that, through it as through no other means given to us, we are again and again given to understand who we really are and who we're ever summoned to become. Especially through the prism of the sacrament in which we're presently to share, we're given to see the one great and universal sacrament that is this world itself and, through it, the deeper meaning of all of our life and of the struggles of all human beings to become what they are.

Such, I believe, is the word that we're to hear through our lesson—the word of God that addresses each of us here and now through the all too human words of Paul and of the one standing before you as your preacher. It is the word that calls each of us once again to become what we are, to become what God through Christ has revealed each of us to be through the event of our own individual baptism—namely, one who, being always already accepted by God's boundless love, always already has the possibility of accepting God's acceptance and thus of walking henceforth in newness of life, free from the bondage of the past and open to the gift and claim of the future through the faith that works by love.

Do you not know, then, my sisters and brothers, that all of us who have been baptized into Christ Jesus were baptized into his death? We have been buried with him by baptism into death, so that, just as Christ was raised from the dead by the glory of the Father, so we too might walk in newness of life. So you also, each of you, must consider yourselves dead to sin and alive to God in Christ Jesus. Amen.